Lead

with Your

HEART

Lessons from
a Life with Horses

ALLAN J. HAMILTON, MD

Illustrations by Róbert Farkas

 Storey Publishing

The mission of Storey Publishing is to serve our customers by
publishing practical information that encourages
personal independence in harmony with the environment.

Edited by Deborah Burns
Art direction and book design by Alethea Morrison

Cover and interior illustrations © Róbert Farkas
Author's photograph © Amber Lea Russell, Amber Lea Photography

© 2016 by Allan Hamilton

Storey books are available for special premium and promotional uses and for customized editions. For further information, please call 800-793-9396.

Storey Publishing
210 MASS MoCA Way
North Adams, MA 01247
storey.com

Printed in China by R.R. Donnelley
10 9 8 7 6 5 4 3 2 1

Library of Congress Cataloging-in-Publication Data on file

TO BUD AND ELLIE

---

who taught all of us
that the best way to teach our children
is through how we live our lives

Contents

INTRODUCTION: Walking between Worlds, 9

TEACHING *and* LEARNING

» Find the right place to start. *14*

» The horse is a mirror. *16*

» Teaching is one phase; training is three. *20*

» Bring a new question every day. *22*

» Reward abundantly. *24*

» The benefit of the doubt is a chance for success. *26*

» Let mistakes happen. *28*

» Correct, then caress. *30*

» Back up for respect. *32*

» The feather is mightier than the whip. *34*

» Patience is compassion. *38*

» Cultivate a beginner's mind. *39*

» Are we having fun yet? *41*

» Finish better than you started. *43*

» Look for the breakthrough and seize it. *44*

» Provide a way out. *46*

» Make the right way the easy way. *47*

» Know when to let go. *48*

» It all begins at the gate. *49*

» Escalate out of the comfort zone. *50*

» Agendas hurt the relationship. *52*

» Nagging is the handmaiden of failure. *56*

» Ask, request, demand, and promise. *58*

» The better the trainer, the less the training. *60*

» Training trumps bloodlines. *61*

» Find the way to celebrate. *63*

» Horse whispering means being clearly heard. *64*

» Doctrines don't fail; methods do. *66*

» Patience creates time; time creates success. *67*

» Stutter steps build memory. *68*

» Hesitation precedes understanding. *69*

» A tired horse will eagerly stand still. *73*

» Balance fear and curiosity. *75*

» A windy day can make any horse stupid. *76*

» Learn the ABCs of teaching. *77*

» Wait for the lightbulb moment. *79*

» Back up to perfection. *80*

» Black and white are fine; shades of gray confuse. *82*

» The faster you go, the worse it gets. *85*

MINDFULNESS: Attention *and* Intention

» Never take a day for granted. *88*

» Every moment has meaning. *91*

» Intention focuses energy to effect change. *93*

» Behold the eye. *95*

» Elegance is economy. *97*

» Make it a habit. *98*

» Know how to be silent. *99*

» Timing must be impeccable. *100*

» Cultivate an eye for detail. *101*

» The mind shapes intention, but the body delivers it. *102*

» Clear your mind. *103*

» Drop the reins. *104*

» The horse's reward is peace. *106*

» Horses don't lie; people do. *110*

» Thinking knows; seeing believes. *112*

» A goal is a trap. *113*

» For horses, more than four is a bore. *114*

» Lists grow as time shrinks. *115*

» Stop wondering if it's quitting time. *117*

» Cinch four times; mount once. *119*

» Life is a series of plans punctuated by the unexpected and the unavoidable. *120*

» Equipment is character. *121*

STALKING HAPPINESS

- » Invite the horse into a herd of two. *124*
- » Practice affection. *128*
- » Put love in your hands. *129*
- » Hunt happiness. *131*
- » Seek the heart of gold. *133*
- » Just breathe. *135*
- » Loosen up. *136*
- » Tranquility comes with each turn. *138*
- » Head position tells a tale. *140*

LEADING *and* FOLLOWING

- » Real power is born from stillness. *142*
- » Use your mind, not the lead rope. *146*
- » Get far more with far less. *148*
- » The answer lies at liberty. *150*
- » Master pressure, not punishment. *151*
- » Boundaries define the geography of respect. *152*
- » Find the curve of compromise. *154*
- » Lead by invitation. *156*
- » Partnership is purpose. *157*
- » Greater power comes from less pressure. *159*
- » The lower the head, the better the frame of mind. *160*
- » The lead rope reveals the relationship. *163*
- » Footwork: dominance first, then respect. *164*
- » Horses act out forever, until they quit. *166*
- » Circle for safety. *168*
- » Never take the trail for granted. *171*
- » Leadership is determined by the four Cs. *173*
- » Give credit. *175*
- » SPS: self-praise stinks. *176*
- » Lead with your heart. *177*
- » A physical confrontation is a defeat. *182*
- » Before danger strikes, consider the possibilities. *184*

» Avoid idleness; employ stillness. *185*

» To be heard, whisper. *187*

» Overcome with leverage, not resistance. *189*

» The more a horse spooks, the less afraid he becomes. *191*

» Leaders assume the risk for all. *193*

» Loyalty is never convenient. *195*

» Horsemanship transforms. *199*

ENERGY *and* EMOTION

» Combining energy and emotion is a choice. *202*

» To know when to release is to know why. *205*

» Energy is duality. *206*

» The ground is closest to the truth. *208*

» Energy is sticky. *210*

» Grow beyond instinct. *212*

» Rhythmic movement is predictable energy. *214*

BREAKING THROUGH

» There is no best way. *219*

» To conquer problems, imagine solutions. *220*

» Don't fix problems; change them. *222*

» Tackle small problems before they become big ones. *224*

» Try the 180-degree solution. *226*

» Love is never the problem. *227*

EPILOGUE: There is still time for the predator to turn to the herd. 229

Acknowledgments, 231

WALKING BETWEEN WORLDS

AS A NEUROSURGEON, I have spent my adult life working inside the human brain with a scalpel. While that experience gave me a unique perspective on the fragility of life, it is not what made me question my own drives and instincts. No, it was working with horses that showed me a path to becoming a better person, husband, and father. Horses taught me that my self-centeredness and materialism arose from my fundamental nature as a predator. They showed me that I was driven to conquer the world because I was afraid to trust it.

Predatory animals must devote themselves to seizing opportunities and exploiting advantages, and we humans personify that attitude. Even when it comes to the fundamental physical parameters of our world, we exhort ourselves to "seize the day" and "manage" our time. We insist that space represents a "final frontier," something to be conquered and claimed. We look out into the depths of the universe with the same naïveté that the conquistadores and the pioneers demonstrated when they faced unexplored territories. Our first instinct is to try to possess it and tame it, not to truly, simply dwell in it. We want to be "out there" rather than "in here." We see the challenge and the struggle as existing outside ourselves rather than within.

Horses see things differently. They are large and powerful animals and can, at times, be intimidating up close, but they are the prototypical prey species. They offer us a practical method to see meaningful alternatives to our own voracious way of life. When we spend the time to see the world through their eyes, we can visualize a path to transform our predatory appetites. They challenge us to undertake the journey of mastering ourselves rather than everything around us.

Teaching without preaching, horses lead by example and employ the lessons of experience. They epitomize immersive learning at its best. And they challenge us with their formidable size and strength to bring results through collaboration rather than by force. Horses have developed their own compelling models of fairness, forgiveness, and leadership. They have acquired a group identity, a consciousness not as singular beings but as members of a family, a herd. They see themselves not as individuals in the isolated context of "me" but as relatives in a family in the broader framework of "we." And they derive a powerful and gratifying sense of inclusion from it.

Horses share resources for the benefit of the herd. They are a wise, gentle species that eschews the notion that might defines right. While stallions with their reproductive imperative come and go, the alpha mare endures as herd leader. Because they understand what it means to be hunted, horses have the most profound appreciation for the benefits of peace. They yearn for harmony, kindness, and tranquility; they crave freedom from anxiety, abuse, and predation. With their nonviolent attitude, horses are a testament that a partnership based on trust is far more productive than one that relies on dominance.

AFTER MORE THAN A QUARTER CENTURY of training horses, I no longer find it easy to distinguish the world of instruction from the realm of philosophy. At times, I find myself slipping from a seemingly trivial detail, such as teaching a horse to lift up his foot, into a much broader principle, such as honoring the connections to life around me. I find myself suddenly unstuck in time and space, able to float from a technical detail to a spiritual insight in a flash. A Zen teacher once instructed his student that to find enlightenment he should learn to chop wood and carry water. In other words, the spirit finds itself in the simplest of actions, not the greatest of accomplishments. Grooming manes and picking hooves is no different from chopping wood or carrying water. The simplest acts can engender the greatest insights.

So it has become my habit to go to the round pen or head out on the trail with a small pencil and some 3-by-5 cards in my pocket. I scribble notes about whatever drifts into my head as I work with my horses. Sometimes it might be a fine point about improving my technique; other times, it's a powerful life lesson. And occasionally, a gust of insight suddenly rushes in with such power that I feel as though it could sweep me off my feet if I can't write it down fast enough. I am convinced that my horses are trying to show me something of value, to help me visualize a different perspective: to see better so I can be better.

This book evolved from the thoughts and images I scrawled on those bent cards, dog-eared notepads, and the backs of faded receipts when I emptied my pockets before throwing my jeans in the laundry. I gathered them, expanded on some, and assembled them so I could slip a copy into my back pocket, go back and refresh my memory, re-inspire myself, as I water my horse or we both rest a spell in the shade of a pine tree.

We are all on a quest for self-revelation. The ultimate homework assignment is to try to become better, kinder, and more loving individuals. The result we hope to see is one of continuing self-transformation. If we halt our search, then nothing lies ahead but stagnation and decay. Each of us must dedicate ourselves to a daily regimen to further self-awareness and growth. Not only is it a habit we need to cultivate, but it must also become our passion.

TEACHING *and* LEARNING

Horses and other herd animals teach us that we share energy between our own individual consciousness and the larger context of the cosmos. That ebb and flow is an energetic conversation teaching us something about ourselves. We cannot be good teachers if we are not good learners. If we haven't learned, we have nothing to teach.

FIND THE
RIGHT PLACE
TO START.

▼

Each person is a unique individual in time and space. Each of us has our own history, our own weaknesses and strengths — some things at which we can succeed easily and others at which we fail miserably.

Even over the course of the day, you wax and wane. You are a different person now than you were when you woke up this morning, even though you have the same driver's license. You can tackle some things with more energy in the morning than in the evening, and vice versa. Sir William Osler, one of greatest teachers in the history of medicine, divided his students into "roosters" and "owls" to account for some learners who came roaring out of the starting blocks first thing in the morning and others who worked better burning the midnight oil.

Horses, too, possess well-developed psyches. Every time we work with a horse — as handler, owner, or trainer — we must ask ourselves: Have

I earnestly looked for the right place to start this particular horse for this particular task at this particular moment?

Imagine that you are in kindergarten. I am your teacher and it's my job to teach you to read. So I plop down a copy of Tolstoy's *War and Peace* in your lap and say, "Start." There's no way you will succeed, no matter how many times I ask. But then I may say, "Today is simply and utterly devoted to just one thing: the capital letter A." Now I have given you a task at which we are guaranteed to succeed as a team.

Like humans, each horse has a unique learning style and speed. He might be better at sidepassing and jumping when he is full of piss and vinegar in the morning, and better at ground-tying when he's tired in the afternoon. Or, you might find it tough to teach ground-tying in the evening when your horse wants to get back to his stall for the dinner bell; in that case, your best bet might be a switch to the morning for ground-tying lessons.

I have had students accuse of me of cheating because I teach my horse ground-tying when he's so pooped he barely wants to move. It looks like cheating because he succeeds so easily, but rearrange the letters in "cheat" and you have "teach" — and teaching means finding the right time and place to make it as easy as possible for your horse to succeed.

Also keep in mind that just because a task was easy yesterday does not mean it will be easy every day and every time. Think of each encounter with your horse as a unique point in time and space where you can maximize the potential for partnership. Every horse is trying to show you "Yes, this is how we can succeed" or "No, this is where we will fail." It's your job, as his partner, to look for those places where you and he cannot fail.

THE HORSE IS A MIRROR.

▼

MASTER, WARRIOR, *SENSEI*, HORSEMAN: these words are synonyms that connote single-minded awareness, focus, discipline, and self-mastery. The search for mastery requires us to become brutally honest with ourselves without feeling defensive. It calls us to cut deep into our own psyche. It carries us to a threshold where we will confront uncomfortable vulnerabilities and inconvenient truths. And on that threshold, we must truly wrestle with ourselves.

Horsemanship demands truth. Nothing less. We can't hide much from a horse. He sees through us with disarming candor and directness. No matter what we reveal about ourselves — carelessness, impatience, self-centeredness — a horse will forgive it, let it go, and move on.

Why is receiving this honest assessment of ourselves so important? First, because it is so rare. Second, because lies present such powerful obstacles along our path to self-transformation. The most holy tenet of partnership is trust. The more we want to devote ourselves to strengthening our partnership with our horse, the more he will insist that we get to work on ourselves, to dismantle all the defensive mechanisms we have

"The basic difference between an
ordinary man and a warrior is that
a warrior takes everything as a
challenge while an ordinary man takes
everything as a blessing or a curse."

Carlos Castaneda, *The Wheel of Time*

assembled, and to earnestly confront our own issues. In that regard, the horse serves us as a powerful mirror, allowing us to reflect deeply on our own problems and see ourselves as we truly are. He accepts us — warts and all. He asks: When are you ready to do the same?

The notion central to all horsemanship is that it is never about the horse. It is always about us, about how we either create issues or react to them. When the problems start to seem complex or stubborn, we need to stop. It means we are close to a new revelation. That is where the turmoil is coming from. There must be a moment of torque before there is traction, resistance before the truth emerges. We must relax, reconsider, and rejoice: another eye-opener about ourselves is right around the corner. That is how self-revelation works: turmoil begets insight.

The horse willingly offers himself as a companion on the path to awareness. His mirror lights the way.

Gender Generalities

The term "horsemanship" is fraught with problems. First, it is ironic that it uses the male gender because more women actually pursue and practice horsemanship than men. Second, no gender-neutral term exists to describe the practice or practitioner of horsemanship. Thus, while we have actors and actresses in the acting profession, there are no such gender distinctions in the realm of horsemanship.

To be both clear and economical in this book, we will generally call the human "she" and the horse "he," unless the context clearly calls for something else.

TEACHING IS
ONE PHASE;
TRAINING IS THREE.

▼

T HE DANGER OF LEARNING THROUGH REPETITION is that we'll take something new and exciting and allow it to diminish into dull, rote practice. This will happen unless you cultivate your beginner's mind for the task. Putting on a new outfit, for example, may be exciting the first time — jewelry, belt, shoes, and the rest of the accessories. Eventually, though, it will become a boring, tedious routine each morning.

If you pursue impeccable intention — a spiritual term meaning "pure motives" — in each step of the process, however, you will see that every task is worthy of mindful attention. This revelation manifests itself in the three phases of training: *teaching, consolidation,* and *practice.*

The *teaching or learning phase* is the most challenging for the human, who must lead the horse to the correct answer. This phase requires finding his individual, personal starting place. From there, the lessons proceed in deliberate and custom-tailored steps, applying the least amount of energy to provide the horse with motivation. This is also the phase that calls for the most impeccable release, where the right answers must be easy for the horse to find and the wrong ones difficult. The teaching or learning phase separates the master horsemen from the rest. It calls for the greatest clarity of heart, mind, and intention in the human, and the highest level of patience and empathy for the horse.

The *consolidation phase* depends largely upon repetition and a gradual smoothing out of all the steps. This calls for a keen eye to see how one step of the task eventually blends into the next as we draw out the release further and further from the initiation point. This phase also puts a premium on release, but it is less critical than in the teaching phase, where releases, even at the slightest try, are what guide the horse to success. In the consolidation phase, a smooth release starts to make the horse's movements and responses more fluid and relaxed.

The last phase is the *practice or maintenance phase*. Now the skill, task, or maneuver is very familiar and recognizable to the horse and part of his armamentarium of behaviors. This last phase places a premium on elegance in execution. At the same time, the horse must have some accountability, so the handler must remain vigilant for breakdowns in technique or less-than-genuine effort.

In life, we tend to go through the same phases. At first, a new experience or relationship is a novel adventure: the learning phase. Then we begin to organize things into routines and we enter the consolidation phase. Finally, the routines become plodding habits or drills: the practice phase.

Even if it is the one-hundredth time you put on that outfit, immerse yourself in being mindful of every step in the sequence. Even the simplest task is worth performing with elegance and economy.

BRING A
NEW QUESTION
EVERY DAY.

▼

HORSES HAVE UNCANNY ABILITIES, and one is the knack of sensing when a problem or question is weighing on our minds. Don't ask me how they do it. I suspect we give away many details about our emotional state through the energy we transmit. Horses, however, want to help.

Often, if I simply keep a query foremost in my mind, a horse will offer me a surprisingly astute, metaphorical response to it. I am in the habit now of trying to formulate it aloud as a question: "What is on my mind?" Then I answer it aloud.

One evening, for example, I came home from a board meeting at the hospital where we had discussed a building I was most eager to see built. The project had derailed, however, and was put on hold. Not the end of the world, but it left me unsettled and sad.

The meeting was foremost in my mind as I approached my horses, and I wondered why it troubled me so, shifting my whole energetic center. I entered the round pen repeating aloud the question over and over, "Why am I so blue? That's the question I need help figuring out."

Remember, horses speak to us energetically; we must grasp their answers through symbolism and metaphor. On this evening, I started working a horse in circles in the round pen, just to warm him up. I loped him once or twice around on the rail, asked him for an inside turn, then had him lope off in the other direction. And repeat. At each turn, the horse was sloppy and sour, cutting a corner of the round pen before each departure, leaving me feeling stupid and frustrated.

In the round pen, each turn is a matter of timing: drawing the horse off the rail, then putting energy on the side of his face to push the forehand off in the other direction, and, finally, directing pressure on his hindquarters to help depart in the opposite direction. I wondered why his turns were so sloppy, why they were falling apart. I could see that I wasn't in the right position to put pressure on his eye to turn his forehand quickly enough. I simply was not prepared to be where I needed to be.

Then it dawned on me: the turns were a metaphor for the meeting. I was upset with myself because I wasn't ready to defend my plans for the building. And now I wasn't where I needed to be, so the horse's turns fell apart like the anticipated building schedule.

Allow your horse to guide you to the answer. The signs can be subtle: a head shake, going to sleep on you in the middle of a session, not turning with you. You must tell yourself: "The horse is offering an answer; I need only to decipher it."

We apply this technique in life, too. Often we walk around with a question burdening us. We must put the question out into the universe as a specific query. Now the universe sends back answers — but only to those who are prepared to hear its language.

REWARD ABUNDANTLY.

▼

É TIENNE BEUDANT, a French 19th-century horseman and cavalry officer, said of horse training: "Ask often, settle for less, and reward generously." These words hang on a banner above my barn door as a daily reminder. With horses (and, alas, frequently with people), we are not vigilant about welcoming opportunities to praise and reward.

We become so fixated on tasks and outcomes that we forget the real purpose of teaching our horse is to help him succeed in life, at every step. So my own axiom has become: *Pause. Pet. Breathe.*

Pause is to remind me, first, to slow down. To deliberately stop myself, to be mindful enough to recognize that my horse has done something to please me.

Pet is to encourage me to show affection, to take a moment to actually stroke my horse and physically reward him.

Breathe is to prompt me to mindfully *relax* and take a deep, audible sigh to help me lower my energy state.

Pause, pet, breathe is a motto to ensure I express gratitude to those who try to please me, or master a skill, or overcome a hurdle. It is a mantra that reminds me to praise with every cleansing breath I take.

So often I see even the most accomplished riders in the world reach down and slap their horse's neck. I understand that horses are big creatures, but why slap to show affection? To my way of thinking, our horse's hide is very sensitive. So my rule of thumb is: *Don't slap a horse any harder than you would your own face!*

The real purpose of teaching is to help our student succeed in life.

THE BENEFIT OF THE DOUBT IS A CHANCE FOR SUCCESS.

▼

WHEN MY HORSE SONNY WAS YOUNG, he slipped in a fast-moving current and almost drowned, and ever after, water spooked him. Any water! There were times when I swear even a thimbleful would send him into a serious spook — a pedal-to-the-metal flight reaction. So I started working with Sonny using manmade puddles. I dug up a corner of my arena and hollowed out a big depression, covered it with a tarp, and flooded it with a hose. The result was a mega-puddle.

To get Sonny through such a trial required great patience. With each step — literally — I had to apply escalating energy to prompt him. So I got in the habit of always expecting that he'd have to struggle; in fact, in retrospect, I probably set him up by always anticipating that he would need my "goosing" to help him through the puddle.

One day, though, my boot got caught in a fold of the tarp as I started to enter the water. My timing was thrown off and I wasn't in position to drive Sonny forward. And guess what? He just walked into that pond. Turned out I subconsciously expected him to fail. I had grown accustomed to a modicum of energy with each step. What I really needed to do was back off and see what he was motivated to do on his own. My bias about Sonny had blinded me to the possibility that he could ever go into a puddle of his own accord. If it weren't for that twisting boot, I would never have discovered how much courage Sonny could really display.

This is a life lesson. If we expect frustration, disappointment, or even sadness, then those expectations *will* shape the outcome. We want to give ourselves the benefit of the doubt and assume things will go perfectly.

Believe that events will unfold just the way we plan. Have faith that the genuine concern, love, and kindness we exhibit to others will be acknowledged and returned. Expect life to pleasantly surprise you — because when we anticipate that our student will fail, we then apply too much energy.

That is unfair, even destructive, because the horse becomes accustomed to a "heavy hand." It makes him dull and unresponsive, and susceptible to anxiety. When we start each trial with the softest of energies, we offer a full spectrum of slowly escalating response. With each attempt, we give our horses and ourselves a chance to reach perfection. We never want our biases or prejudices to stand in the way of gaining that experience. To be fair and just, always offer your horse every opportunity to shine.

LET MISTAKES HAPPEN.

▼

TRIAL AND ERROR ARE VITAL COMPONENTS of the learning process. None of us is perfect and we all make mistakes in judgment, management, and technique. Without these errors, we would never learn. There is nothing so frustrating as someone correcting us *before* we have made a mistake.

Horses are no different. They must also be allowed to make their own mistakes. We cannot crack our dressage whip or smack our lariat against our leg just because we think our horse might slow down by the gate as he lopes past it. We cannot correct for what is *going* to happen, only for what already *has*. We must admonish our horse only when he actually *does* slow down by the gate.

Whether teaching horses or children, we must shape corrections around actual mistakes, not expected ones. If we put out the intention that our pupil will make a mistake, he usually will. In contrast, if we anticipate achievement, we'll get it.

If we are sending a horse over a jump, for example, we must picture him clearing it. If we worry about when he launches or how high he holds his frame, then we cloud our vision with mistakes instead of a clear image of success.

Regard mistakes with a bit of a smile. They are the requisite steps of learning. Approach them with playfulness and humor, because each mistake carries us closer to wisdom.

"Experience is the name everyone
gives to their mistakes."

Oscar Wilde

CORRECT, THEN CARESS.

▼

B Y THEIR NATURE, HORSES ARE NOT AGGRESSIVE. They are peace-makers. By and large, they are inclined to pull their punches a little, holding back — especially with humans. Before getting aggressive, a horse will *always* give the human a warning of what is coming. Too often, though, we miss or ignore those signals. If and when a 1,200-pound horse decides to get physical with a 150-pound human being, it is a life-threatening situation.

Occasionally, judiciously — and only in self-defense — you may need to discipline your horse with an outright smack. Do it quickly, decisively, and, yes, forcefully. And *get it done* — once and for all. You will be doing yourself and your horse a great favor. Make sure you darn well drive that horse away from you as vehemently and clearly as you can. Show that you mean it.

A reprimand should be a single event. If you must keep reprimanding your horse repeatedly, you are doing something wholly wrong. And never, ever deliver the blow in anger. Summon a great deal of energy in the shape of a physical blow and make it absolutely clear to the horse that he should never make that aggressive decision again. But make sure there is no anger whatsoever in your heart — that this is a correction and not a state of mind.

Here is an equally essential companion adage: Always follow a whack with a hug or a rub, to indicate forgiveness. The caress, in the same place where you delivered the blow, turns the whack into a correction. It is now in the past, and there are no hard feelings. The sooner you pat, the sooner your whack is forgotten. If you follow hard with soft, no resentment will take root.

My mother had a wise rule: Never go to bed mad. As a kid, this made me realize that no matter what mistake or misbehavior I had committed, at bedtime it was all in the past and I was sent off with a big hug and a kiss. Even at work, if I have to reprimand one of my staff, I always try to think of a nice compliment I can give the person before we leave the office. Correct, then caress.

BACK UP
FOR RESPECT.

▼

B ACKING UP IS A TIME-HONORED METHOD of recognizing nobility and acknowledging status. It is also a powerful technique to de-escalate potentially aggressive situations. It immediately reduces the pressure exerted by one subject on another. It is not a retreat as much as a respite, offering some breathing room.

With horses, backing up has special significance because it is not part of their everyday repertoire of movements. Of course, they can manage it *physically*, but *psychically* they are creatures dedicated to forward movement. They will, however, back up if properly taught on the ground (and later under saddle).

When a horse willingly yields to your energy and backs up, it is a sign of respect for your personal space. In the horse's mind, if you are the leader of this little herd of two, you must be able to demarcate and defend your personal space.

Ensuring that your horse will willingly back up away from you is the single most important method to develop his respect. Not only might it help safeguard your safety, but he will also be more relaxed knowing you will always clearly indicate to him when and where he is invited into your space. Respect is the foundation of partnership. You cannot go forward until your horse goes backward.

When personal spaces draw close, there is usually a build-up of oppositional forces: *chi* colliding with *chi*. Backing up conveys to animal or human an instant message: our desire to reduce any oppositional energy.

In the *human* social domain, when you sense resistance building, try backing up physically. There are two good reasons for this. First, a message registers with your counterpart on a subconscious, visceral level: I wish to diminish confrontation and ease tension.

Second, stepping back is a physical way of releasing tension in the body. The maneuver lets you regain a clear head and a stance of impeccability.

The world of horsemanship is full of paradoxes, and here is one. Getting your horse to work on backing up is one of the fastest methods to get him to make quick progress. We should never mistake his backing up for backing down. It is not; it is a horse's way of demonstrating respect.

When you sense resistance, try backing up.

THE FEATHER
IS MIGHTIER THAN THE
WHIP.

▼

AS HUMAN BEINGS AND PREDATORS, we are fascinated by displays of power — even violence. Be it the rise of another terrorist leader, the latest school shooting rampage, or the newest darling on the football gridiron, we are unwillingly mesmerized by displays of might.

The horse, however, is captivated by a different notion of personal power: namely, strength that never asserts itself in excess. Given his enormous size and strength, virtually no physical restraint a human being could impose could contain him if he set his mind to resist it — neither a bigger shank in his bit, nor a tighter tie-down, nor a sharper set of spurs will do the trick. The only reason such devices even appear to give some semblance of command over a horse is that he allows it. The irony is that the more restraint we try to impose on our horse, the more he will question whether to trust our predatory nature.

"Life does not turn out the
way it . . . 'should.' Life turns
out the way it does."

Tracy Goss, *The Last Word on Power*

Our only reliable tool for controlling our horse is our mind. We must abandon physical restraint and find ways to offer him a greater degree of freedom to respond and cooperate of his own free will. When we can prove to him that we are relying on his trust in our partnership to let us teach him, our work will become more productive.

Not every horse can start off with every freedom. Some must earn it in increments, but even they need to sense the work is moving toward greater freedom and not increased restraint.

Trust is a power, too. It takes patience to tend and cultivate it, but it can then become potent in its own right. The difference between trust and might is that might never allows freedom of choice. It compels by force and, in the process, diminishes the subject with every decision that is made for the horse.

Trust, on the other hand, provides freedom of choice for each individual in the relationship. In any close relationship — be it marriage, parenthood, friendship — each individual party must safeguard the other's individuality, enhancing liberty and responsibility with every decision. If, at every turn, trust is expressed, then both parties will remain committed to grow together.

Trust allows freedom of choice for both parties.

PATIENCE IS COMPASSION.

▼

G OALS BRING OUT THE PREDATOR IN US. The price we pay is losing that sense of infinite, uncompromising patience that every horseperson, every human, needs. Patience helps us safeguard our integrity and compassion, and restrains our ambitions and agendas. Patience helps us guard against polluting our intention.

Our actions while working with a horse should focus only on the matter at hand and the energy shared between horse and rider. When you exhibit anxiety or frustration about making the horse perform or accomplish a specific objective, you lose your focus.

Once, at a clinic, I was so intent on demonstrating a point that I jumped onto my horse's back without realizing that he was sound asleep. I was worried about what my audience was thinking of me, rather than about what my horse was doing. I got bucked off for my troubles — right in front of the grandstand.

CULTIVATE
A BEGINNER'S
MIND.

▼

WHEN I TRAVEL TO A DISTANT PLACE to hold an equine clinic, I depend upon the horses provided for me. The day before the clinic, I usually want to see them — not because I care what they can or cannot do, but because I want to get a feel for each one's personality.

I always start with a careful greeting, rubbing the horse's shoulder and walking away. I want to see how he holds himself. I want to see if he stands there or moves toward me when I demonstrate that I am not aggressive.

Next, I take him for a walk. I ask nothing of him, but approach him as a total novice. I want to see how he reacts without pressure, without an expert touch. Then the horse begins to show me his propensities. Does he crowd me? Does he stop readily when I stop? When I change direction, does he travel with me?

I observe the students in the actual clinic as well. Too often, they are looking for one cookbook-style recipe for how to fix a problem, rather than simply starting to work on a solution.

For example, a participant might ask, "How do you make your horse stop walking forward when you stop walking forward?" Of course, I could just say, "Do this and do that and he'll stop walking forward." But that would be of little use to the student and her horse in the long run, because it provides no real personal experience to help with the next issue they confront together.

Instead, I exhort her to stop her horse moving any way she can. I pose the problem like this: "Say your horse was about to step on a land mine, how would you stop him?" Then she just dives into the problem with a beginner's mind, unfettered by rules, and finds a solution.

The beginner sees a world of possibilities. She is not limited by what *should* happen, but is ready for what *might* happen. Her mind is not clogged by expectations; she simply experiences, without deliberation.

How do you cultivate a beginner's mind when working with a horse? Don't approach him confident in what you know, but instead keep an open mind about all the things you don't know. The humble beginner is far more receptive than the established expert.

ARE WE HAVING FUN YET?

▼

WE SPEAK OF HOW MUCH A HORSE HAS "between the ears" or how willing he is to please. But how well a horse learns reflects more on our ability to teach than on his ability to learn. Instead we should question how much a teacher puts between the horse's ears or how willing she is to satisfy the horse.

The rule of thumb is this: If our horse is not learning smoothly and progressively, then we are not doing something right. We need to go back and reevaluate what and how we are teaching. Are the steps in our technique small enough for him to grasp easily? Are we ensuring he can succeed at each milestone? Finally, we have to ask: Is our horse having fun?

Marshall McLuhan, the 20th-century guru on media and communication, once said: "Anyone who tries to make a distinction between education and entertainment doesn't know the first thing about either." Learning should be entertaining and educational for both human and horse. If the horse isn't having fun and succeeding, chances are good we aren't either. When we are no longer learning, we're drilling. Then it is time for us to go home and rethink things.

Whether for horses or for people, three things distinguish a lesson from a practice drill:

1. It adds to an existing fund of knowledge and skills.

2. It provides engaging, immersive entertainment.

3. It connects us to the world around us.

The next time you take a lesson — whether in how to braid your daughter's hair, can your own peaches, or cast a fly line — think about the experience as it happens. Does it add? Is it fun? Does it connect? If not, change it. It's your session: you're the only student and the only teacher.

FINISH
BETTER THAN
YOU STARTED.

▼

MASTER TEACHERS PRACTICE how to flow into and float out of each session. They are mindful of the condition of all the participants at the start and take responsibility for how they feel at the end. Careful stewardship of relationships means understanding the arc of every encounter.

A good example of this is when starting a lesson with a horse. At the beginning of every session, the horse has his own agenda and set of distractions. The handler must allow the horse some time to orient himself and assess his surroundings. As his mind and eye come into alignment with the handler's, the lesson gets under way. The session must have a progression to it — a beginning, middle, and end. The handler carries the horse through this arc with intention, and the horse should finish the session more focused, relaxed, and successful than when he started. Find the perfect moment of his accomplishment, and finish there. Knowing when to quit is an essential ingredient of good horsemanship.

LOOK FOR THE BREAKTHROUGH AND SEIZE IT.

▼

E ACH WORKING SESSION HAS ITS OWN PACE. There is no set time or length of practice required for the horse to learn a task, because every horse is different on any given day. We must have a feel for how quickly he is acquiring the skills and when and where the breakthrough will occur.

That breakthrough is the point where he has moved through learning the task and is beginning to consolidate it into an acquired skill. Too often, we keep driving and drilling the horse to get him to perform the task perfectly. Learning comes through practice, but that practice always works better when there is a short interval (no more than a day) between the learning phase and the consolidation phase of the task.

The breakthrough may not happen at the end of the 20 minutes we've set aside for teaching. Instead of paying attention to the clock, pay attention to the progress of the horse. When the breakthrough comes, it is time to quit and a great place to start the next day.

I have noticed that the same thing applies to working with any student. As parents or teachers, it is our responsibility to find the place to quit where success is most tangible. I always admire the teacher who lets class out early because he or she feels the students have reached the right place to dismiss the class, not because the class bell went off. Although we try to pigeonhole our experience and constrain it with schedules, rarely do human affairs fit snugly between the hands of the clock. Reach the end of things and finish on a high note.

At the moment of breakthrough the lightbulb goes off. The horse gets it, and his response takes on a palpable momentum. You feel as though you're suddenly rolling downhill. Everything becomes easier and more graceful. There's a thrill as everything tumbles into place.

PROVIDE A WAY OUT.

▼

PREY ANIMALS INSTINCTIVELY LOOK FOR A WAY OUT, a path of escape. For every maneuver we ask a horse to learn, we must also incorporate into the task an escape route. This is vital because the path of escape is the natural route along which the horse will move to seek release from pressure. We can use this route to help him successfully complete the task.

When we teach a horse to initiate a side step, we turn his nose to face the rail. As we exert pressure on his flank, the only route open to him is off to his side, so a side step becomes his best escape. We've used his natural desire to flee to shape his behavior.

In every interaction, every conversation, we must provide the other party with a way out. Don't corner them. Don't crowd them. Always give them an opportunity to get out and save face. Offering an escape route is a subtle way to demonstrate respect and generosity.

MAKE THE
RIGHT WAY
THE EASY WAY.

▼

L EARNING A TASK SHOULD BE LIKE SKIING. Doing the right thing
should feel like turning our skis downhill into the fall line, moving
with gravity. We pick up speed effortlessly. And when we do the
task the wrong way, it should feel like turning uphill. We expend a great
deal of effort to get anywhere. We just cannot wait till we can turn back
into the fall line.

It should be the same way for our horse. The right thing is easy to
accomplish, but the wrong thing is work and feels more difficult, like skiing uphill. Imagine getting a horse to turn inward as he circles the round
pen. Whenever he turns inward, all your pressure comes off. It feels easy
to him. But when he turns outward, you run to cut him off and you make
him pick up speed. Turning outside is work. Turning inside is not.

The easier we can make it for a horse to find the correct response, the
faster he will learn the task. Right is easy. Wrong is work.

KNOW WHEN
TO LET GO.

▼

S UCCESS COMES, ALMOST PARADOXICALLY, when the teacher turns the student loose. When we first teach a horse to do a task, there may be quite a bit of trial and error and corrections large and small. But as he "gets" the concept and learns to carry out the task with fluidity, we can let go and encourage him to accomplish the task for himself.

It is a big mistake to nag him but an even bigger sin to do it at the end of a task as much as we did at the beginning of it. As our horse becomes proficient at the undertaking, we must be keen to remove ourselves from his awareness as much as possible and assume a position of detachment. He is then free to carry out the task as independently as possible.

The ultimate example is working a horse at liberty where we, as horsemen, are standing silent at the epicenter of command but he is the sole source of action. The final fruit of success is when the horseman feels superfluous, providing only the initial interaction while the horse accomplishes everything on his own.

IT ALL BEGINS AT THE GATE.

▼

S WINGING OPEN THE GATE IS CROSSING THE THRESHOLD of awareness. It is the chance to ask the horse for attention and respect as
we enter a sacred working space and time. It is also an opportunity
to reinforce our own commitment to stay focused on the horse and avoid
other distractions.

Minutiae and worries frequently sidetrack us from the larger purpose
of life — namely, to stay connected to something bigger than ourselves.
Our purpose is to seek greater clarity with our horse so we can expand our
partnership.

We can apply those same qualities to the larger context of our lives.
The gate is a metaphorical invitation to be mindful and vigilant about our
behavior. Our work begins as the gate opens on the circle of life.

ESCALATE OUT
OF THE
COMFORT ZONE.

▼

T HE STATEMENT "Escalate your pressure when your horse looks too comfortable" may sound as if we have it backward or wrong. But escalating, in this context, means gradually increasing the amount of energy you apply to your horse. And when should you escalate that energy? When he is still ignoring the energy you have already applied.

The whole point of putting energy on the horse is to help him search in earnest for release. As an example, say the handler wanted her horse to pivot to the right on his hindquarters. Since the horse will always move away from a focus of higher energy to one of lower energy, the handler must exert enough pressure the left side of the horse so the move to the right feels more comfortable.

The handler thus escalates slowly, step by step. She can start by wagging a finger at the horse or shaking the very end (the popper) of the lead rope. No result? Escalate the energy. Maybe introduce a gesture of the whole hand or shake the last 6 inches of the lead.

When is enough? The handler must watch her horse. If his head comes up and he starts to crane his neck to the right, he's getting uncomfortable. At that moment the handler's job is to maintain her pressure at that level until the horse finds release by stepping to the right. She does not need to escalate any further. She is seeking to motivate the horse, not to punish or traumatize him. If he's shying away at a given level of energy, he's motivated. We do not keep upping the ante on him.

Now we help him to find the release. Release needs to be visualized as *the fastest possible decrease in energy we can engineer*. It takes practice to figure out how to drop your energy to zero in an instant. It takes time, but great horsemen generate a tremendous, almost palpable release. Our job is to make that path to the comfort zone as natural, easy, and accessible as possible.

"Things are entirely what they appear to be — and behind them . . . there is nothing."

Jean-Paul Sartre

AGENDAS HURT THE RELATIONSHIP.

▼

NOTHING DESTROYS A RELATIONSHIP FASTER than an agenda. Having a goal in mind makes us try to extract something from our partner.

As human beings, we are exquisite predators, hardwired to focus on achieving our objectives. We are driven to reach our goals and receive our rewards; without them, we feel deprived of closure. We ask ourselves: Where are we going? The task can seem pointless and we can feel cheated without the reward.

Tom Dorrance, one of the fathers of the natural horsemanship movement, wrote: "In working with people and trying to help them with something, I find it isn't easy for me to get them to work in the area where it seems they need to work. They keep trying to work at the end result."*

Goals are our undoing.

Intention is not ambition. Intention is creating a focus of attention where being in the moment is the only reason for summoning the energy.

* Tom Dorrance, *True Unity* (Word Dancer Press, 2003).

"Look to the essence of a thing,
whether it be a point of doctrine, of
practice, or of interpretation."

Marcus Aurelius, *Meditations*

Fostering intention without ambition is the only way to ensure that working with the horse is autotelic, that the activity itself is its only objective.

Our horse reminds us: When we focus too hard on the goal, we lose sight of our partner. We must learn to establish an objective without attaching any value to it. It comes? It goes? It does not matter. We must embrace partnership without goals.

The only arrow that cannot miss is the one that is never aimed.

NAGGING IS
THE HANDMAIDEN
OF FAILURE.

▼

N AGGING IS A SIGN that we are doing something wrong. By nagging, I mean repeatedly asking for a response without a deliberate, stepwise increase in the energy we apply. Nagging can ruin a horse because he learns simply to ignore our signals. It indicates one of two things. He does not have an inkling about what we want. Or — by far and away, more common — we have failed to escalate.

Nagging will crash any of the three phases of training. It can be particularly destructive in the teaching phase and can make a horse lose respect for us as his handler. Nagging is unfair to him because there is no opportunity for release and no chance for success.

The best example I know where novices seem to routinely sink into nagging is when driving a horse around the round pen. When students are asking the horse to accelerate to a more rapid gait (say the trot to the lope or canter), there is tendency for them to run around after the horse's rear end, shaking the training wand or dressage whip behind him. The problem is, they just keep shaking the whip with the same amount of energy — repeatedly. Naturally, if the energy level stays the same and the horse does not respond, then he is being taught to ignore the stimulation and pressure being applied.

That is why nagging is so destructive for a horse. It seems like the nice thing: don't increase the amount of stimulation on the horse. But in the end, he has been done a gross disservice. For myself as a parent, my best teachers about the dangers of nagging were my own kids. It always seemed to focus on cleaning up their room. I would bark at them six or seven times to "clean up this room." The problem was, I continued coming in and scolding rather than increasing incrementally the pressure I applied. For example, I could have said: "If I come back here in fifteen minutes and the room is not tidy, there will be no playing on the computer tonight." The threat of depriving my kids of computer and video game time would have escalated the energy I applied to the situation. Instead, I kept nagging at them with the same volume (same frustration, different words perhaps).

What I was actually teaching them was that it was okay to ignore me whenever I yelled at them to clean up their room because nothing had happened the preceding four times when I had raised my voice. So think of nagging as this: it is a dulling of the horse's (or child's) attention — a systematic desensitization — as the very moment when we really wish to increase awareness.

If we ever find ourselves nagging, it is a sure sign we must immediately stop whatever we are doing, regroup, and reevaluate.

ASK, REQUEST, DEMAND, AND PROMISE.

▼

WHEN WE ASK A HORSE TO LEARN OR ACCOMPLISH A TASK, we ask in four steps: *ask, request, demand,* and *promise.* Always in that order. We never skip a step. We create increments for every task and every horse we have. Ask is featherlight. Request is obvious. Demand is insistent. Promise is declarative.

The example I like to use is a boss asking for a report:

Ask. "Do you think you could get this back to me by Tuesday?"

Request. "Make sure I get this no later than Tuesday."

Demand. "I had better have this back on my desk no later than Tuesday."

Promise. "If you don't get this back to me by Tuesday, you're fired."

While teaching, we usually use only the first three phases because the promise phase is harsh and should be used rarely, if at all. Nevertheless, you must have these four phases clearly mapped out in your mind as you undertake a task. For the hot-blooded, flighty horse, the amplitude must be turned way down. For the horse that is slow to respond, maybe a bit lazy, turn it up and be more forceful. Each step is a deliberate escalation in energy. There should be a measured interval during which one level of energy is applied and the horse provided with ample time to respond.

Finally, especially in the teaching phase, *do not escalate* if the horse is uncomfortable. If he is uncomfortable, find a way to help him find an answer instead.

"This is what you shall do: Love the earth and sun and the animals, . . . argue not concerning God."

Walt Whitman

THE BETTER THE TRAINER, THE LESS THE TRAINING.

▼

HORSES MAY BE AS MUCH AS A THOUSAND TIMES more sensitive to energy and body language than we are. For example, when I am riding my horse, how does he know the difference between when I am turning my head to the left to look at something, like a mule deer in the bushes, versus turning my head to the left because I am asking him to head off in that direction? I have no idea how, but every horse I have ridden reads me properly. I must be doing something subtle with my body posture or muscular tension that communicates my intention.

A good trainer learns to trust that sensitivity in the horse. In the teaching phase, the handler will often exaggerate gestures to help the horse understand the task. As he begins to consolidate the learning and move into the practice stage, the human's movements become subtler, almost like hand signals. At the end, the only movements needed may be limited gestures with the hands or even the fingers.

TRAINING
TRUMPS
BLOODLINES.

▼

MOST PEOPLE BUY WAY MORE HORSE than they will ever need. Except at the most refined levels of professional or national-level competition, training makes a far greater difference in a horse's personality and willingness to work than does his breeding. Genetics tell you about a horse's capacities; training defines what he can actually do.

Most horses' genes are so generous that the average trainer will never reach the practical limits of a horse's potential. The sheer athletic ability of even the average horse is barely touched by the demands of most trainers or riders. For example, few people have ever ridden their horse at full throttle, a wide-open gallop. To imagine that power, think of a Thoroughbred race; then remember that most of us are content with a lope.

Similarly, most people are content to see their horse wheel around on the hindquarters or forehand. But compare that with the maneuvers (the "airs above the ground") carried out by Lipizzans in the Spanish Riding School or those executed by the horses at the National Reining Horse Association Futurity.

People spend way too much money on buying their horses and way too little on training them. Most training never even begins to challenge a horse to the point that his physical and genetic limitations are holding him back. Don't worry about your horse's bloodlines; worry about training, training, training.

FIND THE WAY
TO CELEBRATE.

▼

THERE IS ALWAYS A BREAKTHROUGH. Every day. It is the handler's or owner's responsibility to look for it and celebrate it. That may also be the place to quit — finish on a high note — or it may be the place to push through a little bit more from the teaching phase to the consolidation phase. My rule of thumb: If it has been a struggle getting there, celebrate and quit.

We cannot depend on others to tell us when to celebrate. When we feel a sense of accomplishment, we should enjoy it. We determine when we are a success. Too many times we stand by and let others pass judgment on our actions. Don't. It is only for us to decide what we will honor and when we will rejoice.

HORSE WHISPERING MEANS BEING CLEARLY HEARD.

▼

THE TERM "HORSE WHISPERING" is meant to refer to natural horse-manship methods that use energy, pressure, and release — the horse's own language — to teach. Nothing about the technique, however, is meant to be an actual whisper. The methods should shout out the meaning loud and clear.

Sometimes people confuse horse whispering with being soft and gentle, never firmly asking a horse to perform a task. No, it's not that. Horse whispering is asking clearly, in the horse's own energetic style of body language, and using as much energy as it takes to help him discover the correct response.

It is whispering because the message sent by the handler or rider is unequivocal. It's black and white. The volume of the voice means nothing; clear commands mean everything. For example, when I squeeze my calves to tell my horse "move out," it always means "move out" and I expect a prompt response within one second or I will apply more energy (squeeze with my heel or my heel with a spur). The goal is to be clear and unequivocal in the cues.

What dulls a horse's sensitivity is inconsistency and doubt. For example, a rider may keep squeezing for three or four seconds. Twenty minutes later, she might squeeze three or four times and then resort to using her spurs. Consequently, in her horse's mind, there are times when a squeeze means "move out" but there are also times when it doesn't, when it has come to mean that the rider will simply ask again.

It's called whispering because it means I am committed to teaching my horse without physical pain or coercion. It's called whispering because it means I am devoted to giving my horse the benefit of the doubt and always asking with the smallest possible stimulus. It's called whispering because I am committed to giving my horse enough time to respond of his own accord. It means I have dedicated myself to finding the least amount of energy that motivates my horse.

So in that sense, it is soft, like a whisper. I might be able to just touch my horse with a feather to get him to move out, but it is always about ensuring he hears me loud and clear.

DOCTRINES DON'T FAIL; METHODS DO.

▼

F EW THINGS ARE MORE NONSENSICAL than insisting that there is only one way to do things. Anyone who claims to know the way all horses should be handled, doesn't. Those who insist that their way is the best way just have not been around long enough to know there are lots of "best" ways.

The problem with any doctrine is that it insists on "one size fits all." It does nothing to encourage the horse owner to evaluate all the doctrines out there and apply just those parts that are pertinent and helpful to a horse at that moment in his physical and mental development.

Think of doctrines and methods pragmatically, as nothing more than tools you are putting in your toolbox. The more tools you have at your disposal, the easier it will be to make precise repairs and adjustments in your horse's training.

PATIENCE CREATES TIME; TIME CREATES SUCCESS.

▼

"**G**IVE YOURSELF A YEAR TO GET THE JOB DONE" is a useful adage when working with a horse. By going through that little mental exercise, you slow down. You are more willing to see tiny — sometimes glacially slow — baby steps as the real successes they are. Giving yourself plenty of time to reach a goal or milestone means you are far less likely to blow your integrity and compromise your partnership with your horse.

Patience is the anvil of success, where the horse's behavior is carefully shaped and gradually refined. The more the teacher slows down, the faster the horse seems to learn. Practicing patience is the key to developing impeccable intention.

STUTTER STEPS
BUILD MEMORY.

▼

MEMORY — HOW ANIMALS LEARN NEW BEHAVIORS — is a complicated physiological process. It is all the more difficult in horses because they have so little transfer of sensory information from one side of their bodies and brains to the other. It is thus very common to discover that when you try to pick up where you left off the day before with your horse, he seems to have forgotten it all.

Relax. That is why the teaching phase must last at least a few days and the consolidation phase of learning can last a week or two. In essence, we need to provide the horse with plenty of opportunities for repetitive practice — stutter steps — to make the learning take hold and cement itself into his muscle memory. Just remember: The more days you take off from working with your horse, the more likely it is that your horse will forget. Repetitive practice creates firm, sustainable memories.

The good news about horses is that they are a bit like elephants: once they have learned something well, they rarely forget it again.

HESITATION PRECEDES UNDERSTANDING.

▼

A REALLY GOOD PITCHER ONCE TOLD ME, "If I am pitching a no-hitter, I prefer that no one tell me and just let me finish the game in peace. Otherwise, I start to worry about the hits more than the pitches. I lose my edge because I am no longer pitching fearlessly."

Patience and mistakes go hand in hand. The truth of the matter is, we learn better from correcting our mistakes than from never making them at all. In fact, I find that when everything is going flawlessly, a general anxiety emerges about not wanting to slip up.

As perceptive handlers or riders, we should search for mistakes. At the threshold of a making an error, we can often see our horse hesitate for just an instant while deciding what is the right or wrong thing to do. Be vigilant for such a moment of hesitation. Don't correct your horse, but rather let the moment play itself out. You can practically hear him thinking through the problem. If you rush in to help at that moment, there is no growth on the horse's part. It only fosters dependency.

He will look to us to provide cues and clues as to what is right or wrong. Naturally, we will coax our horse at the beginning of teaching him any task. But there is a transition stage where he begins to ask himself, "Hey, I wonder if this is what I am supposed to do?"

This is where we want to let things hang in suspension for a few seconds. This is where he makes strides in term of his own learning. We have to give him the opportunity to think for himself.

"Knowledge can be communicated,
but not wisdom. One can find it, live
it, do wonders through it, but one
cannot communicate and teach it."

Hermann Hesse, *Siddhartha*

A TIRED HORSE
WILL EAGERLY
STAND STILL.

▼

I T IS IMPOSSIBLE TO TEACH A HORSE TO STAND STILL if he already is. How do we reward him with a release from pressure if he is already released? The answer is: First we must get him to move.

The easiest way is for us to move him in a circle. We then bring him into us at the center of the circle, lead him off, and then quickly pick a spot. We set his feet so he is balanced in a stable position on all four feet. Now we can walk around him once or twice and then rub him, breathe, and casually walk off. Reset his feet and begin the process again. Then we can gradually increase the stimulation around the horse while reminding him to stay put.

We want to frame our lessons with proper timing. The moment to teach your horse to stand still is not when he is full of piss and vinegar. When then? When he has come back from a trail ride and is hot, sweaty, and tired. That is the right time to work on standing still because that is precisely what he wants to do. Fatigue is a great motivator because, as prey animals, horses are inherently energy-conservative. When they are tired, standing still has great meaning and value to them. All we need to do is distinguish clearly between when we are asking him to move and when we are asking him to stand still.

A guiding principle of working with a horse is always to seek any factor that will give us an edge, that will help us motivate him to think of the right thing to do. The best handler is the one who gets creative in her search for motivational allies.

BALANCE FEAR
AND CURIOSITY.

▼

EVERY ONE OF US IS A UNIQUE blend of strengths and weaknesses and fearfulness and curiosity. It is an important part of wisdom to understand that we had no control over who would become our parents or what our genetic makeup would be. Nor during our formative years, could we, as children, exert much control over our environment.

Part of wisdom is finally accepting that you must learn to love yourself for the person you are and stop wondering what happened to the person you wanted to be.

It is no different with horses. A horse's personality plays itself out along a spectrum. If something spooks him, and then he discovers it is not really after him, he wants to turn around and figure out what it is. We want a horse with enough common sense not to plunge blindly into a situation; at the same time, once he has ascertained it is safe, we also want him to be curious about what lies ahead and move forward to investigate.

The right blend of caution and curiosity makes for a great horse. Too much fear, and we end up with a flighty horse. Too much curiosity, and we end up with a rash one.

A WINDY DAY CAN MAKE ANY HORSE STUPID.

▼

WHEN THE WIND GETS BLOWING TOO HARD, it becomes an enormous distraction for a horse. The breeze that was so full of useful information is overwhelmed by unpredictable gusts. His nose and ears can no longer accurately localize scents and sounds. Where's the dog? His smell was centered over there by the tree, but now he seems to be in three different places at once.

A strong wind means an impending sensory overload. The horse has so many movements and rustles to pay attention to that he can't sort out what needs his focus and what does not. Everything in the environment becomes animated and loaded with energy, frenetic and chaotic and unsettling. It is the very opposite of the peace and tranquility he seeks.

Under these conditions it is best to cut the ride short or simply take a day off. That said, there are times when you may want to use the wind and its distractions to test your horse's attention and ability to focus under adverse conditions. Just choose the circumstances and location wisely.

LEARN THE ABCs OF TEACHING.

▼

T HE ABCs OF TEACHING HORSES are really not that different from those for teaching humans. A is Awareness and Abilities. We must be able to see where both we and our horse need to start, faithfully assessing his and our own abilities so that we initiate the lesson from a point of comfort. Always start with something he is familiar with and then slowly let the lesson shift to the unfamiliar. This is an enormous confidence builder for him.

B is for Body and Bravery. Remember, your horse is always reading your body, not your mind. Always make your body speak clearly and succinctly. The word "bravery" is a reminder to reward your horse for every act of bravery — for every instance when he takes on a task with which he was unfamiliar or hesitant. Never betray that sense of bravery by forcing him too far outside his comfort zone. The best thing he could say about you is this: "She never asked me to do a thing that I didn't feel confident about and ready to do." In the end, you want your horse to value his own courage.

C is for Concentration and Confidence. Always focus on the horse and his needs. The best way to describe the intense concentration of working with a horse on the ground is that "I feel and hold him with my eyes." I am always aware of when my eyes are on him and when they are not. At a very fundamental level, accomplished handing comes down to how and when you look at your horse. Under saddle, on the other hand, I contain him with my legs, my seat, and stance. I'm aware that the state of union arises from my body against his.

The second C is for confidence. Not the horse's. Ours. Nothing throws off a horse as much as a handler or rider who does not know what she is asking for. To that end, we must become fluent in our techniques before we apply them to our horse. Let's say we plan on working our horse with a lariat. Maybe it's been a while since we handled a rope. We need some time to reacquaint ourselves with how it handles, tosses, and coils back up. Once we're in there with our horse, we know we must deliver.

WAIT FOR
THE LIGHTBULB
MOMENT.

▼

A S YOU TEACH YOUR HORSE A NEW TASK, you will be encouraged that he is getting better and better at it. You assume the job is almost done and soon he will be wonderfully proficient at whatever it is. The next day, however, he seems to have forgotten everything you taught him. It's as if his brain has just gone blank.

Don't get discouraged. It is simply a developmental stage in a horse's learning process, where he suddenly seems to remember nothing. Keep at the task patiently and confidently. Just as suddenly, the lightbulb goes on in his head: "Oh, yeah, I know how to do all this."

The human equivalent might be a senior moment when we simply lose our focus for an instant. It may be a reflection of some sort of memory consolidation going on in the equine brain. Do not get angry. Be patient and tell yourself that this is a common side effect of how horses learn. He will recover from his amnesia.

BACK UP TO PERFECTION.

▼

W HEN I BEGIN A CLINIC, I ask people simply to shift their horses around. I'm looking for the horses who move a lot around their owners and the owners who move a lot more around their horses. I look at how much eye the horse gives his handler as a measure of how much attention he is paying her. But what I find to be the most telling is how well the horse backs up for the handler.

Backing up is not necessarily a natural move for horses. They are designed to move forward and sideways. While they will back up in the wild, it is not their first choice. A horse that will readily and snappily step backward out of his handler's space is a respectful horse. One who will yield backward only with tremendous pressure has to learn the meaning of personal space and boundaries, and we will not get much further with his lessons until we get that concept worked out.

There are eight fundamental times a horse should back up:

- When I apply pressure on his nose.
- When I apply backward pressure on his halter via the lead rope.
- When I shake his lead rope at him.
- When I wave my training wand at him, either up and down or side to side.
- When I stand alongside my horse's shoulder and lean slightly into his space, against his shoulder.
- When I am walking in front of him and step backward.
- When I push on his chest.
- When I lean back in the saddle and bring my hands toward my body.

Finally, if he won't back up readily when you are on the ground, he will never do it under saddle.

BLACK AND WHITE ARE FINE; SHADES OF GRAY CONFUSE.

▼

W E ALL STRIVE FOR CLARITY IN OUR LIVES — in our relationships, in our communication, and in our thought processes. Clarity entrains action and helps define boundaries and behavior.

Horses look for clarity. They seek people who will communicate their intention clearly and unequivocally. A perfect example is boundaries. I am struck by how many clients have big, pushy horses that are following right up close to (almost on top of) their owners. These are what I call "back-pocket horses" because they always give me the feeling that they would be happiest jumping in my back pocket.

Whenever I work with a back-pocket horse, I slow everything down. I don't jerk on his lead to get him out of my space; instead, I work on backing up. Then, when I am sure this concept is quite clear to him, I ask him to stand at a specific distance from me — say 6 feet. Every time he moves his feet toward me and crosses that imaginary circle, I react and back him up beyond the 6-foot barrier.

Eventually, that horse understands that if he creeps forward — even 1 inch! — over that boundary, I will react. As long as he stays more than 6 feet out, my body is soft and drained of energy. This lets him know release lies at the 6-foot line and beyond and he will receive more pressure when he steps closer. In fact, my energy level goes up in accordance with how quickly he tries to reduce the distance between himself and me.

What makes this work for the horse is that my boundary is exactly the same each and every time. My reaction is the same. It's black and white. Horses love clear, declarative instruction. What confuses them is when I say, "Well, I'll let you get by with 4 feet today." Or "I'm really feeling blue this morning, so I would like to hug you and we'll forget the boundaries."

Those shades of gray kill a horse's discipline. All that sloppiness and sway in your guidelines leave him confused. Oftentimes, students ask me why I am so picky about where my horse stands or whether he moves a couple of feet. It's because I care enough about him to be crystal clear. Black and white.

I often think of the boundary exercise when I see mothers struggling with their children in the grocery store. I struggled with my own, so it is very familiar. The child is whining and asking for candy at the checkout line. Mom says, "No. You'll ruin your appetite. It's close to dinnertime." Child whines some more, and more loudly. Mom says, "I said no." Child keeps at it. Mom finally gives in with the admonition, "But you have to promise me you'll eat all your dinner or there will be no dessert! Do you understand?" The child nods earnestly as he downs the Snickers bar, but he really doesn't understand.

"No" didn't really mean *no* because after two "no's" came a "yes." If Mom thought his appetite would be ruined, why make him promise to eat all his dinner? How could he if his appetite is wrecked? What started off as a confrontation over a candy bar ended up becoming an issue about dessert. Shades of gray everywhere; it is no wonder that the next time, the child cannot figure out precisely what is expected.

So often in life, when we ask for something from a spouse, a boss, or our child, we do not clearly define our requests. We are surprised that our spouse is not more romantic because we asked him or her to be more "attentive," or we are disappointed that we got a change in title but no salary increase or corner office when we went in asking for a promotion.

The ability to make a clear request or demand is a valuable tool. Clarity in thought and deed takes practice. The horse reminds us that there is grace and elegance in clarity.

THE FASTER
YOU GO, THE WORSE
IT GETS.

▼

H ASTE NOT ONLY MAKES WASTE, but physical urgency also com-
plicates and magnifies problems. There is truth to the notion "If
you want to hurry up, slow down."

This is why we start off a lot of sessions at the walk before we apply the
lesson at the trot or the lope. Horses are prey animals. Naturally, as they
speed up, they get more reactive and their bodies stiffen. If we see a horse
tightening up and getting more rigid and fearful, we want to work at a
slower gait until he loosens up and grows more comfortable.

When we work our horse under saddle, slower is softer and looser. We
do not ask him to move up in gait until we are sure he is relaxed and fluid
in the slowest gait. At the first sign of trouble, we downshift to a slower gait
to work out any problems.

As a rule, if it is bad at a slow gait, it gets even worse at a faster one. Slow-
ing down allows clarification.

There are two notable exceptions to this rule. The first is when a horse is "cross firing," or on the wrong lead at the lope. There, speeding up the horse's gait to a faster lope will usually address the problem.

The second exception is in the earliest phases of ground work. Do a lot of work at the lope, because it helps to purposefully tire out the horse a bit. Do this in a measured and deliberate fashion. You do not want to exhaust the horse or have him gasping for air. You do want him a bit more motivated to look for release. That means you accentuate the difference between when your energy is active and when it is passive.

MINDFULNESS
Attention *and* Intention

None of us will get where we want to go in life without a warrior's mentality of awareness and discipline. Mindfulness, the sense of living on the keenest edge of reality, is not born from simple knowledge but springs from a desire to engage in our life's purpose with passion, clarity, and freedom.

NEVER TAKE A DAY
FOR GRANTED.

▼

I F HORSES ARE TRYING TO TEACH US ONE THING, it is to become genuinely mindful and aware in our everyday lives. They are the embodiment of a peaceful soul, anxious to please, to serve, and to carry their share of the relationship. They team up with us.

In return, they expect us to be vigilant, to look out for them, and to lead the herd safely. Riding down the trail as horse and rider, we are an amalgam of prey and predator mind, of fast feelings and fast reactions, of piercing intellect and energy matched with striking power and elegance.

To ride down the trail on horseback is to enter a state of grace. This rare opportunity is available only to those of us who love and ride horses. It is through a profound partnership with our horse that we experience the heightened consciousness known as horsemanship.

So let's pinch ourselves from time to time. Give a prayer of thanks to the natural world that has afforded us this unique opportunity to gain access to the heart and soul of an animal as noble as the horse. Let us pray we can be inspired to be worthy of the one who carries us.

"Easy is right. Begin right and you are easy. Continue easy and you are right. The right way to go easy is to forget the right way and forget that the going is easy."

Chuang-tzu

EVERY MOMENT HAS MEANING.

▼

HORSES TEACH US THAT EVERY MOMENT has energetic significance. For example, you may think you are simply leading your
horse back to his stall. Your horse, meanwhile, is enlivened by all
the energy in every motion, noise, and smell around him. He will notice
if your dog is lying sleepily on the ranch house porch or single-mindedly
chasing a squirrel up a tree. The energy of that dog's state of mind reso-
nates with him.

Think of your horse as constantly "pinging" his environment to see
what energetic foci are out there that might be relevant to him. Since he
is reading every moment's energy, no moment is neutral to him. So while
the walk back to the stall may seem like a perfunctory chore to you, it is
filled with energetic interplay for your horse. Learn to study your world as
closely as your horse studies his.

The horse never lives in an idle moment. He is either teaching us something or learning something from us. He lives in constant conversation with energy crackling in every waking instant. Look upon your horse as a teacher who constantly reminds us that the universe is seeking to engage us — whenever we're ready to dance.

The horse never lives in an idle moment.

INTENTION FOCUSES ENERGY TO EFFECT CHANGE.

▼

ALL LIVING THINGS POSSESS, ABSORB, AND TRANSMIT ENERGY. We all understand this concept, yet few of us commonly apply it in our daily lives.

Energy is like sunlight. You can place a magnifying glass in a sunbeam and focus the light so sharply that it heats up and ignites a leaf. The capacity to create heat was always inside that sunbeam, but it took the magnifying glass to make it able to produce fire. Until you saw the effects of focusing the sunlight, there was no way to know that such an energetic transformation could occur.

The vital energy we all possess, our *chi,* is analogous to sunlight. Intention is how we assemble our *chi*, the magnifying lens that concentrates our energy to create change in our lives. When we discipline ourselves, our *chi* — our vital energy — is unaffected by our need to see a desired outcome.

Applying energy through intention is the direct link between our horses and ourselves. Intention allows us to focus on what was already primed to occur in the horse. It happens because he was ready to make it happen; our intention is merely the catalyst.

No matter how well one holds a magnifying glass, one cannot capture the sun's rays at night. By the same token, intention can assemble energy only for what is ready to take shape. Working with horses encompasses the art of waiting for what was impossible to become possible.

The horse is uniquely sensitive to the way we transmit energy through our gaze, posture, and gestures. He is constantly sampling our energy to decipher our message. In this way, he becomes a gifted mentor to teach us how to move, focus, and apply our energy. Every twitch of his muscles teaches us the alphabet of energy. Then he waits for the poetry to come. The horse demonstrates how to shape our energy to connect to all the life-forms around us.

Becoming mindful of energy allows us to communicate better. For example, there are two kinds of conversations: the ones where we are listening and the ones where we are speaking. Active listening means lending our energy to the conversation without opinion or interruption. We do not look for "holes" in the dialogue where we can say what we want; we do not wait for the speaker to grab a breath so that we can edge in our own words. All we do is listen with every ounce of our attention.

When we discipline ourselves to become mindful of our own energy and the energy around us, as attentive listeners we learn to apply impeccable intention.

The horse is the *sensei* who exhorts us: "You see now that the world is alive with energy. Engage it and live your life accordingly."

BEHOLD
THE EYE.

▼

T HEY SAY THE EYES ARE THE WINDOWS TO THE SOUL. We must become students of the eyes in order to perceive the state of mind behind them. We can see in them the flash of anger, the warmth of compassion, the steely gaze of rejection, the softness of love, and the swift shadow of sadness — without a word spoken, before the impulse comes to dissimulate and hide emotion from view.

Horses' eyes are worth study. It is vital to evaluate the quality of the eye when buying a horse. A horse's eye should be large, round, and kind. Looking into it should be like staring into a dark, clear pool that drinks in all the movement and detail beyond it. A horse's mind is a peculiar balancing act between caution and curiosity. The horse's eye should have an intelligent inquisitiveness to it, combined with a flicker of caution.

We must learn to read the attitude our horse's eyes express. For example, his eye will grow dull and lose its curiosity and engagement as soon as he is bored, and especially if we fall into the trap of redundancy in our work with him. By the same token, caution will shift to hesitation and even outright anxiety if we ask too much of him too early. Learn to recognize how his eye relaxes when he understands what we are asking of him.

When he feels genuine attachment and affection for us,
his eyes say: "We belong to each other."

Note the peculiar softness in his gaze when he trusts us. When he feels genuine attachment and affection for us, when his eyes say "We belong to each other" — that is the highest compliment a horse can ever pay us.

As students of the eye, we reach out to read emotion in human and animal alike. Focusing on the eyes lets us register the feelings of others without necessarily having to process them. If we make the effort to see deeply, we will also deepen our capacity for empathy.

ELEGANCE IS ECONOMY.

▼

P ICTURE A MATADOR. A great one brings the fans out of their seats by keeping his feet still and making the bull turn perilously close around him. His stillness grabs the crowd's imagination.

It is the same with horsemanship. The more economical your movement, the more impeccable your intention becomes. You must discipline yourself to value your own expenditure of energy as much as that of your horse. The softer your approach, the lower the amplitude of energy you need. The more elegant your approach, the less movement required to transmit your energy.

Energy emerges in a still mind, in a still body. Tranquility within and without. Life holds few secrets greater than that.

MAKE IT A HABIT.

▼

T RAIN YOUR HORSE FIVE DAYS A WEEK — no matter what horse, what week, or what year. Horses need consistent practice. When we go for a run or to the gym to work out, it is just lost time and effort unless it becomes a habit. Same for a horse. Sure, we may be out of town or it is a long holiday weekend, but make it happen so that the horse will get worked five days out of seven. If you cannot work him, find someone you trust to help.

Consistency is the key. Some days, you may have abbreviated sessions of 10 or 15 minutes, but do get your horse to run through his paces (specifically, his exercises) regularly.

Learning is the fruit of consistent repetition and practice.

KNOW HOW
TO BE SILENT.

▼

SILENCE ENTHRALLS A HORSE. Since he is the essence of nonverbal communication, a good working session is punctuated only by a few clucks and kisses and "Atta-boys." The handler or rider understands that silence is filled with meaningful release and reward.

Words are for humans; silence is for horses.

TIMING MUST BE
IMPECCABLE.

▼

YOU CAN DEVOTE AN ENTIRE LIFETIME to deciphering the magic of a flawlessly clear and precise release. Timing is everything, but no one is born with it. Three fundamental tenets of horsemanship emerge from the horse's prey nature:

1. The horse's reward is a release from pressure.

2. This release must be impeccably timed, because whatever behavior the horse was exhibiting at the instant of release is the behavior that will be reinforced.

3. It takes time and experience to develop an impeccable release.

A horseman's release becomes the signature of his or her career. It reveals the experience, practice, and discipline acquired over a lifetime to achieve clarity in the letting go of all energy. The horse gains insight through each instance of precise, perfect release.

The mastery of horsemanship rests on this.

CULTIVATE
AN EYE
FOR DETAIL.

▼

GREAT HORSEMANSHIP requires detailed, meticulous observation. The good teachers are devout students of horses. The differences in how horses move, what gifts they have, and how fast they learn are all revealed in tiny details: how soft the eye gets, when they cock an ear or a leg, how tight they hold their lips, how often they lick them.

You can never learn too much about your horse. The more you learn, the better he becomes.

THE MIND SHAPES INTENTION, BUT THE BODY DELIVERS IT.

▼

B REATH IS THE ESSENCE OF ENERGETIC CONTROL. It is the touch-stone of our energetic connection to the life-forms around us. Our thought processes create intention. Our body transmits it. The mind can shape energy through intention, but it relies on the body to make it manifest. This is one of the primary reasons that connecting with horses is a visceral rather than a cognitive experience. When energy is properly assembled, we can feel it long before we understand it. We can work on mindful awareness all we want, but until we feel it, nothing has happened.

It is as if the action is anticipated a moment before it happens. There is a feeling in your gut: "My horse is going to do it this time. I know it."

CLEAR YOUR MIND.

▼

ALWAYS TAKE THE TIME — as you step into the round pen, the arena, or the saddle — to clear your mind. Sigh. Breathe. Focus on your horse. The trick here is to do whatever you need to do to shut down the inner voice in your head and allow yourself to extend your presence energetically out to your horse.

Each of us must learn to shut off our individual "monkey brain" voice in our way. My method is to concentrate on my horse. I try to visualize the individual hairs in his coat. I then picture my own breathing as the wind. I imagine my horse's hairs rippling to and fro with each breath I take. With that amount of focus and visualization, the monkey brain seems to go silent.

I use the same technique when I am trying to listen actively to people. If I focus on their words, their body language, and their gestures, I stop trying to interpret what I am feeling. Instead of internally "verbalizing" what you are experiencing, just feel it and be aware of it.

Remember, you work with your heart, so clear your mind out of the way.

DROP THE REINS.

▼

ONCE I WAS TRAVELING ACROSS THE RINCON MOUNTAINS east of Tucson on one of my all-time favorite trail horses, a great big Quarter Horse named Sonny. We were into some treacherous, rocky terrain when a freakish storm suddenly roared up the other side of the range and closed in around us. In the driving rain and low visibility, I quickly lost my way.

The weather got more frenzied, and I got more anxious. I was seized with fear until I heard a voice say, "Drop the reins." The idea seemed suicidal. But the voice commanded me again: "Drop the reins."

For some reason, I listened. I let the reins go slack across Sonny's neck and let him go. He started off into the heart of the storm and I just hung on to the saddle horn. By God, if that horse did not lead us flawlessly down the mountain, picking his way with steady certainty. Finally, after a long, harrowing descent, his hooves clomped on a small wooden bridge. I knew where we were — 50 meters from the trailhead and right next to the main parking area. We were safely down and off the mountain.

I had to acknowledge that my rational human mind could not cope with the situation, and that Sonny had powers beyond mine. His connection to his environment and his wisdom became my last hope, and trusting something deeper than my own skills became my salvation.

"Can you walk on water? You have done no better than a straw. Can you fly in the air? You have done no better than a bluebottle fly. Conquer your heart; then you may become somebody."

Ansari of Herat

THE HORSE'S REWARD IS PEACE.

▼

A S PREDATORS WE LEARN FROM REWARDS. We seek a prize, a treat, or a bonus to motivate us. We are driven to search, find, and achieve. The urge to pursue, to hunt, links directly to the satisfaction of the reward at the end.

The minds of prey animals are different. They are almost the opposite, in that they seek *not* to be hunted. Life is pleasurable to a grazing animal when there are no threats, when peace prevails. For a horse, life doesn't get any better than being plunked down in the middle of a lush, green pasture. On top of a hill. Surrounded by his best buddies in the herd.

And from his vantage point atop the hill, what does he behold? Nothing. As far as his eye can see, his hearing can reach, or his nostrils can smell, there is not a threat to be found. He can breathe a deep sigh of relief, knowing he is free of any perceptible danger. Nothing is pressuring him in any way.

"It is a paradoxical but profoundly true and important principle of life that the most likely way to reach a goal is to be aiming not at that goal itself but at some more ambitious goal beyond it."

Arnold J. Toynbee

To highlight the enormous difference between predatory and prey motivation, consider a racetrack from the horses' perspective. First they are led to a claustrophobic box. Suddenly freed, they are immediately smacked on the hindquarters by a crop, so they try with all their might to outrun one another. As they run, they may ask themselves: "What is chasing us all from behind? Whatever it is, I don't want it to get me first, so I'm running to the front of the herd." Horses gallop around a racetrack, in essence, because they want to escape and reach the safety and security beyond the finish line.

By contrast, when greyhounds race, they need a mechanical rabbit to chase around the track. Without something to chase, there's no reason to race. It's a diametrically opposed mind-set from that of the horse.

And when the horses burst across that finish line, what is their reward? Relief. They finally gain some peace. Of course, there are wonderful racehorses bred for their love of running. But we are actually breeding them to enhance the basic instinct all horses share — to outrun the others to safety.

HORSES DON'T LIE; PEOPLE DO.

▼

O NE REASON HORSES ARE SO THERAPEUTIC and instructive for humans is that they are nonverbal. Humans lie all the time — about others, to others, and, worst of all, to themselves. For example, there are owners who fear their own horses. They justify their own timidity by describing the horse's idiosyncrasies or their own bad experiences in the past. Yet their body language is shrieking about how terrified they are to handle their own horse.

It is so difficult to address a problem when it is denied or suppressed. The horse can help because he cuts through all that camouflage and obfuscation. He can respond only to the emotional truth surging from the rider.

Establishing that level of candor in one's life is a refreshing splash of reality. It awakens you to the fact that what the horse does is up to you. So what good does it do to try to hide your fear?

Working with juvenile offenders, I've seen gratifying examples of how horses can liberate humans from their own narratives. These adolescents were accustomed to dwelling within their tough, "gangsta" personae. But when these kids were alone with a horse in a round pen, all of that attitude disappeared, because the horse wasn't interested in how they talked or postured, or what gang colors they wore. These youngsters were metaphorically stripped naked in front of their horses, and, for many, it was the first time in years that they could get in touch with who they really were.

The best moments occur when alone with a horse,
because that is where truth abides.

Those kids out of the juvenile justice system discovered that they could trust a horse with their secrets. They could still be themselves and work on themselves. The best moments occur when we are alone with our horse, because that is where truth abides.

Moreover, the round pen is like Las Vegas — "What happens here stays here." It is safe and sacred ground where the horse helps you face the truth. With no judgment, there is no reason to lie.

THINKING KNOWS; SEEING BELIEVES.

▼

HORSES EPITOMIZE THE SLOGAN "JUST DO IT," made famous by Nike, the sneaker and athletic equipment manufacturer. Most people approach horsemanship with too much cognition and not enough ignition. Handling or riding is about moving horses, not talking them to death. It is about physically and energetically pushing them through space as you change your body posture, stance, and position. It is about using the horse's feedback to know what is working and what is not.

Try to avoid thinking too much about the horse. Try seeing and feeling instead. Use a holistic and intuitive right-brain approach rather than a logical, cognitive, left-brain one. When you see the horse physically changing in response to your own energetic changes, you will believe.

With horses, intuition always trumps thinking. Trust the lessons you learn with your heart more than any lessons you think you have learned with your head.

A GOAL IS A TRAP.

▼

GOALS ARE FOR PREDATORS. If you want to trap a predator, give him a goal he yearns to reach.

Objectives are traps that can derail our work with our horses. Setting a goal is always for the needs of the handler or rider and never for the benefit of the horse. For example, no horse says to himself: "Gosh, it would be great if I could complete the trailer-loading training in under an hour!" A goal pulls the horseman's focus away from the horse.

It is not that we should not have goals. Of course you can have an objective or endpoint for a session. The main thing is to avoid becoming too attached to it. Does it really matter if you reach your objective in one hour, one day, or one year? The question should never be "Did we complete the task?" It is always "Did we do we better today than when we started?"

There are only two good cures for this problem.

First, we must recognize the myriad ways in which we unconsciously set goals for our horses and ourselves. The habit is insidious. Ask yourself, "What do I want from this horse?" Invariably, it reveals an implicit goal that you have set for the horse.

Second, you can deconstruct the goal by telling yourself it doesn't matter. That immediately deflates its urgency so you can focus on the horse.

FOR HORSES, MORE THAN FOUR IS A BORE.

▼

A PREDATOR, SUCH AS A DOG, will keep performing a training task over and over because it is motivated by a reward. A dog will play fetch till hell freezes over and never tire of it. Prey animals are different. They are seeking release; a component of irritation and resentment sets in when they are asked to do a task over and over. Horses like their tasks mixed up and varied a bit, or they grow stale.

As a general rule, ask your horse to do something three or four times in a row, and no more. You can come back to the practice again in a minute or two, but in the meantime ask him to do something different that lets him switch gears.

As with most rules, however, there is an exception. If you believe your horse is right on the edge of making a breakthrough in a task, you might want to push on through rather than abruptly switch gears. But, always, gauge the quality of your teaching by the response of your student.

LISTS GROW
AS TIME SHRINKS.

▼

I WORK WITH MY 20-YEAR-OLD QUARTER HORSE SONNY almost every day. We have been best friends for 15 years. My secret nickname for him is "Buddha," because he is like a wise, old, enlightened *sensei*. He stands to the side of the round pen and looks at me as if to say, "Ah, so you think you are ready, grasshopper? We shall see."

Working horses never gets dull if we approach it with the mind-set that it is *our* lesson and not the horse's. As we accumulate experience, we begin to see that natural horsemanship is about immersing ourselves in the partnership. We learn to stop trying to reason everything out and allow our intuition to awaken.

I would have to say that Sonny never really disobeys me. What I've noticed is that when something is off with him, it is because I've slipped somewhere. In other words, Sonny keeps sending me back to look inward.

The only mystery about horsemanship is: Will we give up the quest? Some people think they get so good that there's nothing left. I always ask them two questions: "Has your horse reached the perfection you seek in him as a partner? And have you reached the perfection you seek in yourself?" If they answer "yes" to either of these, I know the lesson is over. If they answer "no," I tell them: "Let's get back to work."

For every task you teach your horse, two more should appear. The horse will never run out of lessons. He will simply get wiser with the passing years.

STOP WONDERING
IF IT'S QUITTING TIME.

▼

L IKE ALL OF US, horses are creatures of habit and routine. Most of us return from a trail ride and bring our horses back to the stable. There we hitch them up, take off their tack, hose them down, and put them up in their stalls to eat. We keep repeating the same pattern. Horses soon think that the moment they turn onto the trail home, it is time to head back to the barn. They pick up the pace, maybe even frantically, so they can get home and start eating.

Before long, we have a bunch of horses prancing and fidgeting half of the return trip back to the barn. We have trained them to expect that work is over and that it's "Miller time" when they can get back to the barn.

We would serve our horses better if we did not put them back in the stall right away. Leave your horse tacked up occasionally, and then take him back out to work some cattle, lope a few laps in the arena, even head back down the trail. Or just let him stand for a while by the hitching post to cool down.

Gradually he will learn never to assume that his work is over. He will no longer anticipate, because he has stopped worrying about whether it's quitting time.

Like most animals, a horse is a creature of habit. If every trail ride ends with getting fed, then that is what he will come to anticipate. If every trail ride ends unpredictably, then he learns to conserve his energy and stands ready for whatever is next.

CINCH FOUR TIMES; MOUNT ONCE.

▼

THERE ARE FEW THINGS MORE DANGEROUS — or humiliating — than having your cinch come loose while you are riding. At best, it is a terribly hard dump on the ground under harrowing circumstances. At worst, it is deadly. So let's get into good habits.

Never take your horse or your equipment for granted. Make it a rule to pull your cinch up tight *four separate times*:

1. When you walk your horse up to the arena to check him out.

2. After you have worked him on the longe line and checked him out in all of his gaits.

3. Right before you put your leg in the stirrup and swing up into the saddle.

4. After you have traveled a half mile or so. As your horse moves out, warms up, and starts extending himself, stop and pull up the cinch a fourth and final time.

LIFE IS A SERIES OF PLANS PUNCTUATED BY THE UNEXPECTED AND THE UNAVOIDABLE.

▼

SHRINKING THE AMOUNT OF TERRITORY YOU CEDE to the unforeseen depends on how carefully you have mapped out your plans. As His Holiness the Dalai Lama pointed out, "Whether you call it Buddhism or another religion, self-discipline . . . [is] important. Self-discipline with awareness of consequences."

Ride down the trail, therefore, with self-discipline and awareness.

EQUIPMENT IS CHARACTER.

▼

E VERY PIECE OF EQUIPMENT HAS MEANING, and every aspect of its design has significance. No one needs to agree on equipment, but each choice should have a justification in the horseman's mind.

I am never satisfied with my equipment. I am constantly designing modifications to my existing equipment: a better-fitting halter, a better-weighted lead rope, a better kind of footing in the arena, a better clasp on the gate. Always question and scrutinize how things are made, the craftsmanship, the design and function. Why is this training wand superior to that one? Why is this set of reins better than those?

Everything should have a reason and a purpose; the handler's tools should become an extension of herself. Whenever I travel to a clinic, I always bring my own halter and lead rope in my luggage. Some people think I am crazy. Why do I insist? Because even an extra ounce or a slight stiffness to that lead rope or halter makes a difference to me. I have spent years perfecting the feel of that rope in my hands. It is second nature to me, like my own fingers. I know its exact length in relation to my waist and my feet and the distance to the horse. I know exactly how big a loop it will make when I swing the end. So when I insist that my equipment be of the highest quality, I am honoring my knowledge as a trainer and my devotion to the horse I am training.

At one clinic I was teaching riders to go over tarps with their horses. The host brought out three small tarps with massive tears and holes in them. She was put off when I said we needed new tarps. "Why do we need new tarps?" she asked. "Because," I answered, "it is hard enough for the horse to learn to walk confidently over the tarp without making him worry about catching a hoof in it and suddenly dragging it behind him."

Lousy equipment betrays a lousy attitude about horsemanship.

STALKING HAPPINESS

Children know how to find happiness: it is at their fingertips. Offer a toy at the airport or a pail at the beach and they are soon filled with passionate purpose. As we mature, we lose that intimacy with our spirit and that ability to dwell in the moment, and joy seems distant and elusive. We can dwell in happiness when we stalk it in the moment at hand.

INVITE THE HORSE INTO A HERD OF TWO.

▼

A FFECTION EMERGES FROM MUTUAL RESPECT. Humans have a physiological requirement for bonding during early childhood development. Without physical attachment, a child simply cannot develop normal emotional and cognitive skills.

Horses have similar needs. Across the equine world, affection and bonding are prerequisites for maturity and mental balance. Early in life, the dam provides affection to the foal. As a yearling, the horse will leave his mother's side and move into the larger context of the herd. In the wild, horses have profound, lasting relationships with their fellow herd members.

But what happens to the domesticated horse, who, more likely than not, was sold and transferred away from what had been the social epicenter of his life since birth? Owners have an obligation to that horse to include him in their own herd. Even if it is just you and the horse, you must create a functional herd of two.

"Happiness is when what you think,
what you say, and what you do are in
harmony."

Mahatma Gandhi

So it should not be a great surprise that horses live for those moments when we share our affection with them. I am shocked when folks do not take the time to show physical affection for their horse. When I query them as to why, almost always the answer is something along the lines of "Well, I didn't want to interrupt anything," or "I was afraid it would distract him."

Distract him from what? What could be more important than showing your horse you care about him? Whenever you have a break, remind yourself to lay a little love on your horse.

PRACTICE
AFFECTION.

▼

I T SEEMS TRIVIAL: PRACTICE AFFECTION. It is not. We must become mindful of opportunities to display affection and approval throughout our lives and our relationships; the horse merely teaches us how to look for such moments.

Why is this such a fundamental lesson? Because as predators we inherently believe that the merit, the reward, the good — call it what you like — lies in our actions, meaning what we embody and what we feel. But in the world of the herd animal, the reward lies in what we engender in others.

The fundamental premise of partnership is affection. If spirituality lies in reaching out to others, then affection is the first step in enhancing that spiritual connection.

PUT LOVE
IN YOUR HANDS.

▼

PRACTICE THE DISCIPLINE OF DIRECTING AFFECTION through your gestures — mindfully infusing your movements with love. How do you do this? The same way you can take the hand of another person — a child, a spouse, an invalid, a dying person — and express kindness and trust. It is altogether different from cordially shaking someone's hand at a cocktail party.

For another example, think of the difference between stroking and brushing your child's hair and preparing your own hair in the morning before work. The former is affectionate; the latter pragmatic. We all implicitly know how to make our gestures convey emotion and compassion. The trick is to understand that the message is more important than the action.

One of the great secret moments of handling, one of the daily devotions, is to show affection for your horse while you groom him. Think of what that means. What do horses do for each other when they are best buddies and standing next to each other in the pasture? That's right, they groom each other to celebrate genuine affection. It is a powerful bonding ritual that cements the herd members together, a ceremony that every horseperson should incorporate into the daily routine.

Show love for your horse at every opportunity. Start with grooming: Practice the discipline of love with your hands. Learn to fill each small act with care.

HUNT
HAPPINESS.

▼

WE CAN ALSO SEEK OPPORTUNITIES where we can exert praise. By doing so, we pursue the Doctrine of Reward: *Find rewards and avoid failures.* The corollary of the doctrine is: *Find success as soon as possible and avoid failure as long as possible.*

An opportunity to succeed is more meaningful and productive than a chance to fail or to reprimand. Success is the stepping-stone to well-being and happiness.

When it comes to horses, praising builds partnership; rebuking and scolding undermine trust. Negative reinforcement has never helped a horse (or a human being) learn. It may prevent an animal from carrying out a certain behavior because he is afraid of punishment or negative reinforcement, but the lesson does not accumulate in his personal repertoire. It is devoid of happiness or any personal sense of success and accomplishment.

Praise, along with opportunity to succeed, is the only path that leads a horse to feeling good about learning a new task. The lesson then takes on an internal value and moves the relationship between rider and horse forward, making the next learning experience that much more appealing.

Stalk opportunities to create success. Our horse will not usually get the whole idea of what we are trying to teach him all at once in an "Ah-ha, eureka"-type moment. Instead, it is more like a lightbulb that flickers, goes out, flickers back to life a bit longer, stutters some more, and then eventually grows steadier until it builds to a bright, sustainable light.

It is easy to get caught up in the routine of schedules, progression, and milestones. We begin to organize the lessons into procedural steps rather than a succession of achievements. A gradual devaluation of success erodes the "fun factor" with our horse.

This also occurs with our coworkers, our children, and our spouses. We put a premium on completing the process and begin to take success for granted. We must yearn for opportunities for success and jump on the moments of satisfaction that punctuate even the most mundane of tasks.

Success and praise are the building blocks of gratitude, and gratitude is the foundation of happiness. So we stalk happiness by building in achievement, praise, and gratitude.

SEEK THE
HEART OF GOLD.

▼

AN ASTOUNDING PERCENTAGE OF HORSES have suffered abuse at the hands of human beings. The disturbing pervasiveness of this cruelty makes me wonder if perhaps we carry a subconscious fear of the animal's sheer size that drives us to hurt him. Because the horse cannot speak out and denounce the perpetrator, the cruelty is not curtailed.

Whatever the reason, humans hurt horses a lot. Often the perpetrator justifies the abuse by claiming it to be a necessary element of training. Violence, however, has no place in handling a horse — or in any relationship with a living thing. Abuse is never for the benefit of the victim, although it is almost always justified that way by the abuser.

An inspirational revelation emerges, however, from all the physical abuse heaped upon horses: the discovery of their profound capacity for forgiveness. No matter how much cruelty a horse has experienced, he will rarely generalize it and hold it against all other human beings. An abused horse would have every right to be defensive and assaultive, but instead, his heart remains open and vulnerable. He is willing to take the chance that the next human being he encounters will be the one who is gentle and kind.

I was once called to look at a horse that had been badly mistreated: the owners had fashioned a terrible bridle made out of barbed wire. The horse, bleeding from scores of small cuts, was removed from the premises and taken to the American Humane Society. The lacerations were easy to heal. But could this horse forgive humans for the mistreatment he had received? I had serious doubts about his ability to be rehabilitated and become safe around people.

To my utter surprise, he quickly proved himself able to evaluate each human being who came along on an individual basis. His mistreatment at the hands of some human beings did not prejudice him against all other human beings. The horse made a decision — the way of the herd — to commit to forgiveness, an ability that I found inspirational.

JUST BREATHE.

▼

WE NEED TO DEVELOP AWARENESS of how and when our bodies assume passive or active energy states. Since our vital energy is most easily condensed into our breathing, learning adequate breath control is the best way to concentrate energy for active alignment and assembly of intention.

Active body language requires the rider to summon energy and let it fill the body with each inhalation. The body becomes tense with energy, which the rider learns to direct and shape with intention. When the intention has adequately focused the rider's energy, it can be brought to bear on the horse. Active energy states inform the horse he must respond to the intention the rider applies to him.

A passive state, on the other hand, requires the rider's body to empty itself of energy and let it drain back into the ground. A deep cleansing breath leaves her body relaxed and empty. Passive body language creates an atmosphere of total release. It puts the horse at ease and asks nothing of him. Exhalation is the essential ingredient of release.

Control of our energy comes with learning purposeful breathing. Peter Matthiessen, a writer who spent much of his life focusing on Zen Buddhism, put it this way: "In this very breath that we take now lies the secret that all great teachers try to tell us."

LOOSEN UP.

▼

WHEN WE CARE TOO MUCH, WE SCREW UP THE RESULT. That is one reason athletes work so hard to stay loose before a big game or event. The rider who cares too much about the outcome of a particular task or session becomes too attached to it. Her intention suffers because of the agenda.

An example that seems to repeat itself over and over in my classes is the classic training lesson of trying to get a horse to cross a "teeter-totter," a thick plywood board balanced over a pole laid on the ground. When the horse steps on one end of the board, it will tilt. As he walks across it, the board pivots on the pole. This lesson allows the handler to help her horse confront the problem of a noisy and shifting platform under his feet. Good practice for trail riding, where ground can crumble or a branch snap under the weight of a horse.

Students often become overly focused on getting the horse across the balancing board during the course of the class. To accomplish that, they are willing to drive him relentlessly — sometimes to the point where he tries to vault dangerously over the entire length of the board. I am far more impressed by the student who first tries to figure out what her horse will comfortably tolerate now. She pulls out the pole from under the board and lays the plywood flat on the ground. If her horse cannot yet handle the noise of the plywood underfoot, then what is the point of focusing on the teeter-totter?

This is where the handler must dwell to benefit her horse. Trying so hard to achieve the objective leaves the horse perilously out in the cold. We can create impeccable intention only when it arises without attachment to the outcome.

The handler must almost take the role of spectator, watching from the outside and letting things happen of their own accord, by their own rules. It sounds almost paradoxical, but the horse will let things unfold at his own pace. The less the handler tries to set that pace, the faster the horse will learn.

TRANQUILITY COMES WITH EACH TURN.

▼

ORSES CAN GET THEMSELVES WOUND UP in an endless spiral of anxiety. The adrenaline builds. The horse starts to run. That pushes more adrenaline into the bloodstream and then, as they say at NASA when the rocket engines get ignited, "the candle is lit." The horse is off in a full-blown panic.

First, allow me to point out that a horse in such a state is potentially a very dangerous animal and needs to be handled with experience and caution. Many owners will advocate just letting him run himself out. My concern with that strategy is several-fold.

First, if the horse is very fit, it could take quite a while until he runs off all that adrenaline. More important, he could get himself hurt or dangerously overheated in such a panicked, fear-stoked state of mind. Finally, the handler or rider is inadvertently building up a behavioral repertoire that includes blind fright.

We always want to teach our horse to think — and not react — his way out of things. Letting him run around in circles in a tizzy is a bad habit. So when your horse starts to get reactive, get him turning and moving his feet. The more frenzied the horse, the more turns we want to demand. This holds true both on the ground and under saddle.

Moving the feet is the answer to panic. That means making the horse circle. Notice that the more frequently you make him turn, the more relaxed he gets. Why? Because we are asking him to focus on his handler and not on his own reactivity. By continually turning, he repeatedly disengages his hindquarters, losing the capacity to "rev up" his engine.

Sometimes the secret to resolving life's anxieties is to turn in a new direction.

HEAD POSITION TELLS A TALE.

▼

A CALM AND ENGAGED HORSE WILL LOWER HIS HEAD and even lean forward. One who is uncertain or leery will raise his head up and lean back on his hindquarters. We want to see our horse pull his head up a bit when he encounters something out of the ordinary but then quickly lower it to investigate. The more time we spend learning to read our horse, the more time our horse will spend with his head down, relaxed and engaged.

There is no finer compliment than going out on the trail with our horse and watching him hold his head in a relaxed, engaged manner throughout the ride. It means we have been so in sync with him that we have let him think his way through the entire ride without needing to react.

LEADING *and* FOLLOWING

We tend to think that leading is somehow inherently better, sexier, and more powerful than following. Nothing could be further from the truth. Leading means taking responsibility for the ones who follow — not so much the power to make decisions about outcomes as the willingness to exercise care and compassion for those who trust us. In the world of the horse, these qualities are embodied in the alpha mare.

REAL POWER
IS BORN FROM
STILLNESS.

▼

T RUE LEADERS ARE CALM, QUIET, AND POWERFUL. They practice
how to summon the least amount of energy needed to do the job
elegantly, without a lot of fanfare or attention to themselves.

Most people expect action and movement during the physical act of
handling a horse. We predators are drawn naturally to action. With horses,
however, real power is the energy born of stillness; great energy is sum-
moned out of quietness.

Sometimes the manipulations of energy used to work with horses can
become so subtle they are imperceptible to the untrained eye. Horsemen
learn they hardly need to move to make things happen around them. If
they perfect the art of standing quietly and peacefully, their very stillness
makes their power irresistible.

For example, a skilled handler does not need to move her feet
much because her energy has become so persuasive it can shift everything around her, including the horse, without resorting to large body

"The inner is foundation of the outer.
The still is master of the restless."

Lao-tzu

movements. To the naked eye, her movements may seem quite constrained in scale. They are not; they are the fullest expression of the least amount of energy required.

As we aspire to improve ourselves, one challenge is to master the projection of powerful energy. We want to apply intense focus with profound restraint and self-control. Tranquility and power must combine in equal measure. Alone, neither can prevail; but together, from stillness, they compel the universe to listen.

USE YOUR MIND, NOT THE LEAD ROPE.

▼

W E OFTEN MISTAKE THE MEANS FOR THE METHOD. For example, we exhort our children to get good grades. In first grade, when our kids ask us why, we answer: "So you can get accepted into a good school." "Why do I need to go to a good school?" they ask. We reply: "So you can get a good job." In reality, getting good grades should simply tell us if a child is well engaged in his or her schoolwork.

The lead rope is a means to an end.

We make the same kind of mistake when we use a lead rope to walk our horse over to his stall or load him into a trailer. We fail to appreciate that the lead rope is a means to an end, a method by which we transmit energy easily and intuitively. The halter allows us to take that energy and mechanically apply it to different parts of the horse's face and neck. Yet an overdependence on the lead rope can interfere psychologically with our motivation and our ability to deepen and refine our energetic connections between our horse and ourselves.

If we wish to push the limits of our own energy, then sooner or later we must learn how to use the lead rope sparingly. To see what happens when we pretend the lead rope isn't there. It is not that we *never* need to use it, but we will never increase our skills if we *always* use it.

Once our horse has learned a task well, we can tuck the lead rope in our belt or pocket and rely more on our energetic intention. Subtlety comes from playing with energy. Can we take a movement that required a whole arm gesture to make the horse respond and convert it to just a flicker of the finger? Can we become so intimately connected with our horse that such a tiny, casual gesture carries enough energy to enable him to respond to it?

When a horse begins to move himself without the lead rope, it is because he's enjoying the relationship. Just as there comes a time when the student will get good grades simply because he or she loves the subject matter.

The first step is recognizing that the lead rope is only an aid — a means, not an end. Part of our reliance on training aids comes from insecurity: "What if the horse doesn't listen to us?" So what? We can always find a way to increase the energy we are applying to him, or we can use the lead rope (or training wand if necessary) to reinforce our request. Don't let the fear of failing stop you from exploring new ways of succeeding.

GET FAR MORE
WITH FAR LESS.

▼

A S HORSEMEN, WE MUST RESIST. If we settle for the fastest, easiest
way to get the job done, we lose out on the opportunity to explore
the energetic limits of refining the task. Instead, we move on
to accomplishing the next task as quickly as possible, unaware we have
missed the point: to get far more with far less. It is not just a matter of how
much power we have; it is also a matter of evaluating how little power we
need to use to get the job done.

We often assume that teaching ends when a horse learns the task. We
don't ask ourselves: "Have *I* learned this task, to best of *my* ability? Have
I pushed myself hard enough to use less and less energy to get the task
done?" If our energy needed to be revved up to "10" to get the job done,
did we stop there, or did we drop back to "5," and then "4'" and so on? Did
we settle for being efficient or did we push on to being elegant?

Outcomes can undo us. We become so focused on a reliable, demon-
strable result that we fail to understand that our greatest strength is also
our greatest weakness. When we are successful with the horse, we want
to return over and over again to that repeatable success, rather than push

ourselves into exploring additional challenges. So being successful also becomes a liability, an impediment to exploring our weaknesses. We demand honesty; we need to know what happens when we are willing to give up the power we have with the lead rope.

"Right thoughts produce right actions
and right actions produce work which will be
a material reflection for others to see
of the serenity at the center of it all."

Robert M. Pirsig

THE ANSWER
LIES AT LIBERTY.

▼

O
NE REASON THAT WORKING A HORSE WITHOUT A LEAD ROPE is
called working him "at liberty" is that it offers us the freedom to
discover where our horse's connection to the lead ends and the
one with our mind begins. We may fear to discover that nothing *but* the
lead connects us. If true, we have not traveled far enough yet.

We are trying to play with energy, not manufacture with it. One of the
greatest sins of our educational system lies in the way it denies students the
ability — the freedom — to play. If one goes into the first grade and asks
the students: "How many of you here are artists?" more than 80 percent
of the students will identify themselves as artists. But ask the same question in the sixth grade and now less than 10 percent still see themselves
as artists. So what happened? The artists got killed off because education
became more about learning and less about playing. Creativity was the
collateral damage.

It is the same thing that happens when we cannot see ourselves playing with our horse at liberty. Let's incorporate more play and less formal
learning into our regimens — be it at school, work, or the round pen.

MASTER PRESSURE, NOT PUNISHMENT.

▼

T EACHING HAS EVERYTHING TO DO WITH PRESSURE and nothing to do with punishment. Punishment is powered by emotion — anger, shame, fear, or frustration. Pressure is powered by pragmatism. It is focused on a specific part of the horse for a specific purpose, at the right moment, to convince our horse to move in the correct way. Our task is to establish the least amount of energy required to get the job done.

Since every horse is different, our mission is to apply enough pressure so that it motivates him to seek a solution, but not so much that he is too anxious to find it.

Some believe that if a little pressure will get the job done, a lot of pressure will get it done faster or better. Nothing could be further from the essence of horsemanship. A good horseman learns to play with energy, practicing to discover how subtle that energy can become.

BOUNDARIES DEFINE THE GEOGRAPHY OF RESPECT.

▼

B OUNDARIES ARE AMONG THE MOST DIFFICULT yet most important things to establish in our lives and our relationships. The
adage "Good fences make good neighbors" could be paraphrased
as "Well-established boundaries make better relationships." It is easier to
protect an established boundary than to create one after a problem arises.

A horse who does not respect boundaries is a dangerous, disrespectful
animal; with him, setting boundaries takes on a visible, direct significance.
It is the handler's responsibility to establish those boundaries and ensure
that the horse respects them.

Meanwhile, it is the horse's nature to probe and test the energetic
fields around any individual, especially those of the humans who work
with him every day. He does this by gradually crowding and encroaching
on their personal space. He is looking for that border where the human's

energy pushes back and creates a palpable resistance. Humans must visualize the space around the horse and create appropriate energetic contact to help him understand the significance of boundaries.

A horse must learn that he enters the human's personal space only when invited. The pushiest horses require the strictest definition of space. They usually belong to owners who have spent too much time trying to get their horses to love them and too little time earning their respect. If one earns a horse's respect, then his love will follow.

The demarcation of boundaries creates the foundation of respect. It separates the private from the public, the friend from the family, work from family life. Clear boundaries require clear thinking and make it much easier to navigate through life.

FIND THE CURVE
OF COMPROMISE.

▼

O UR PREDATORY NATURE MAKES US GO AT THINGS DIRECTLY. We want to take the shortest route possible and move in a straight line. When we introduce ourselves to others, for example, we walk straight ahead, face each other frontally, show our teeth in a ritualistic smile, and then extend an open hand to shake — an atavistic gesture to reassure our counterpart that we do not have a weapon in our dominant hand. That's a predator's greeting; we go straight to our goal.

Prey animals, on the other hand, instinctively avoid direct lines of sight. They want to reduce the odds of being caught out in the open, so they walk along curved, meandering paths, moving from one position of protection to the next.

To make our horse feel comfortable, we walk up to him obliquely, staying in the middle of his visual field. We do not approach him in a straight line but, instead, adopt a gentle curving arc. We greet him at his shoulder, an area a predator would never choose as a point of attack. We avoid staring directly at him but gaze down at the ground, thus reassuring him we have no intention of stalking him.

We stroke him on the shoulder, and then show him our back. This symbolic gesture again sends the message: "We're not hunting you." If we were, we would not have exposed our back.

We then walk away, our back turned, again reinforcing that we want nothing from him. We merely seek to greet him respectfully. Our gentle demeanor follows the curve of compromise.

Teachers often discover that the straight, blunt line of attack and confrontation does not work. The horse shows us that the curve may be the shortest distance to what we seek.

In our daily lives, we must notice when we are creating lines of resistance and when we are creating curves of compromise. Are we creating a situation where resistance engenders more resistance, or are we seeking a way that this relationship can flow of its own accord?

LEAD BY INVITATION.

▼

I F YOU PULL HARD ON A HORSE, THE HORSE PULLS BACK. Pull more, and he yanks back even harder. It is instinctive to respond to force with more force. Both parties expend more and more energy to get absolutely nowhere.

Let's minimize how much yanking we do on the lead rope. Why? Because when it comes to a tug-of-war contest, the horse will always win. We must stop thinking of it strictly as one party winning and/or outsmarting the other. Instead, consider the question: Did we create enough energy consistently to draw the horse with us?

When leading a horse, fight the temptation to meet resistance with resistance. Instead, find a way to invite him to come toward you, to join you in departing. The tension in the lead rope is a measure — a reminder — of how willing he is to follow us. We want to avoid walking away from our horse in a straight line as we apply pressure on the lead; instead, we want to see him moving out without tension in the lead rope.

Excessive force creates fear, resistance, and resentment in the horse — in anyone. Resistance, friction, and shows of strength fuel rebellion. Compromise and communion remain the trademarks of the peacemakers. True power never raises its voice.

PARTNERSHIP IS PURPOSE.

▼

THE PARTNERSHIP BETWEEN HORSEMAN AND HORSE is sacred. Nothing takes precedence over it. Without it, there is no purpose to horsemanship.

This is a deceptively simple concept because at every juncture, the handler must ask: "Is what I am asking of my horse important to *his* life?" Paradoxically, if the answer comes back as, "No, it is *not* important and it is of *no* consequence," the handler can proceed. Be assured there is then no chance the work will take on greater significance than the horse.

Let's put this into human terms. Let's say I am trying to teach my child her multiplication tables. The *way* I teach her the multiplication tables (making it fun, giving her plenty of examples, and rewarding her with praise) is more important than *what* I teach her: that is, the tables themselves. If the learning is fun, then there is no limit to what my daughter can tackle as a task. If, on the hand, I put the emphasis on how vital the math tables are to her pursuit of a scientific career that will lead to financial success, then I lose my integrity with her now, in the present.

I have sacrificed the child that is here with me for the adult somewhere off in the distant future.

In horsemanship, the horse trumps everything, and we must frame our goals in the context of what is best for our relationship with him. When a handler is forthright with her horse, then no illusion or conceit clouds her judgment or detracts from her technique.

GREATER POWER COMES FROM LESS PRESSURE.

▼

POWER USUALLY EQUATES TO GREAT PHYSICAL STRENGTH or high levels of energy. Both rely primarily on mechanical advantage. For example, forcing a horse to his knees because his front leg is tied up is exerting mechanical leverage to make him lie down. Bringing a dressage whip down across a horse's rump is delivering a high level of energy through the mechanical advantage of the lever arm of the whip.

In horsemanship, however, these techniques do not gain the horse's confidence; instead, they make the reactive side of the horse emerge quickly and powerfully. Displays of mechanical strength only drive home the point that the handler still does not trust her intention. As she gains experience, efficiency, and fluidity, she learns to exert the least amount of pressure on the horse to teach him his task.

A quiet assurance descends upon us when we know we can obtain the results we need without resorting to great strength or pressure. Restraint gives rise to respect, respect to partnership.

THE LOWER THE HEAD, THE BETTER THE FRAME OF MIND.

▼

T HE HORSE'S HEAD RISES WHEN HE RESISTS and drops when he desists. It is important to see his head position as a barometer of his own internal emotional state.

Initially, as he is learning, it is not unusual for a horse to elevate his head. This is a natural manifestation of avoidance behavior. We do not need to worry about it but rather simply acknowledge this as an indication that he is still learning (and therefore a bit anxious). When he becomes more comfortable that the task is well within his repertoire, he will relax and his head will come down of its own accord.

Avoid focusing on getting the horse to lower his head; instead, focus on getting him more comfortable with the task. Work on his state of mind, not the position of his head.

"The only man who never makes a mistake is the man who never does anything."

Theodore Roosevelt

THE LEAD ROPE REVEALS THE RELATIONSHIP.

▼

THE LEAD ROPE IS A QUICK AND HANDY WAY to visually assess the relationship between rider and horse. Handlers who are somewhat anxious about losing control usually grasp the lead rope too tightly or hold it too close to the brass. They do not fully trust the horse to make adequate decisions — or mistakes. In contrast, handlers who hold the lead rope too loosely may be a bit uncomfortable about exerting control over the horse; he then wanders aimlessly about, focused more on his own needs than on the task at hand.

The lead should be slack enough to give the horse opportunities to make decisions on his own, but taut enough to exert pressure quickly and judiciously and help him find the correct response. The rope should be confidently present but secure enough that it does not constantly remind the horse of its existence.

Freedom and constraint are difficult concepts to calibrate. The harder we restrain, the more likely we are to trigger the impulse to escape.

FOOTWORK: DOMINANCE FIRST, THEN RESPECT.

▼

ORSES ARE HERD ANIMALS. In the herd, the pecking order is vitally important to everyone's survival. The alpha mare makes the big decisions for the herd. The other horses back up her authority and follow her lead and her orders. There is clear-cut respect from the other horses because the mare has already established her dominance.

The same is true for riders. We must show our horse who is dominant. What that comes down to is: Who moves whom? Whose personal space is more secure?

The feet tell the whole story. If we cannot control the horse's feet and protect our own space, we will not receive his respect. Once we do assert our personal space, he will respect us. The first thing we need to do is create what I call "gravitational pull." The term "gravity" aptly describes the energetic presence that the handler brings to the round pen because it makes the horse orbit around her.

Try this experiment to feel that gravity: Walk into the round pen. If the horse looks at you, walk over to one side of the round pen and turn your attention outside of the round pen. He will begin to feel your presence. If the horse comes over, try seeing if you can stop him just by turning around and looking at him. Once he looks at you, try to get him to turn with you as you walk around him. Then send him off around the round pen, driving his feet as your feet make smaller and smaller circles. Soon he is orbiting around your position. His feet keep moving because your gravitational pull requires it. That dominance — that pull — needs to be implicit in every task and lesson.

I have to say that the best example of gravitational pull I have ever seen was in the White House. I had the opportunity to visit while George W. Bush was president. When he walked into the East Room, his presence seemed to electrify the audience — myself included. I had not expected that reaction. I had always thought President Bush was not the most moving speaker we have had in the office, but, in person, his presence drew the audience in. Each individual in that room had the sensation that the president was talking directly to him or her. That he was there to speak with them.

From the first day entering the round pen, with even the rankest horse, the first thing we must do is show our horse that we can make him move his feet. If we cannot establish control over a horse's feet, then there is simply no hope of teaching him. Without gravity, things just spin off into space.

HORSES ACT OUT FOREVER, UNTIL THEY QUIT.

▼

WE ONCE HAD A PAINT HORSE that was very anxious to get to his food whenever we opened his stall door at the end of the day. It was a bad habit, rude and potentially dangerous — he even once knocked a handler over in his haste to get to the grain.

I instructed all the handlers from then on that, first, they were to hold the horse in his stall by his halter for more than thirty seconds before they could let him eat and, second, they were to take the grain out of his feeder. This way every time he rushed over there was no food there. In the meantime, we put four identical buckets out with feed in only one so that he would be forced to search for clues to figure out where his grain lay.

Despite all of these precautions, he still kept running into the stall. This went on week in and week out with no discernible change in his "rushing" behavior. I was just about ready to get even more aggressive to stop the behavior when it simply disappeared.

Horses can be stubborn, particularly when clinging to a bad habit. They seem able to make us believe that they will never quit their bad habit or reactive behaviors. This is when patient detachment makes the difference. Emotionless energy just keeps plodding along, eroding the horse's habits. In the same fashion, the wise parent ignores her child's tantrums and refuses to let her emotional buttons be pushed. Sometimes the child will persist in apoplectic displays of rage and fussing. The parent must outlast the child, and we as horsemen must outlast the horse. He will always quit, as long as we never do.

We remind ourselves that we have the rest of our lives with our horse and, if necessary, we will keep at it that long — a lifetime. Once our horse sees that we mean business, he will give up. Guaranteed.

CIRCLE
FOR SAFETY.

▼

AS SOON AS YOU ARE READY TO WORK AT CLOSE RANGE with your horse (assuming it is starting off as a rank, wild one), it is time to teach him to disengage the hips.

Start alongside the horse and get him to turn reliably on the forehand. Start by asking for only one step at a time. Work patiently until he is consistently doing a 360-degree turn, with the front inside leg essentially drilling a hole in place as he pivots and his hind legs crossing, one in front of the other.

Once he does that consistently while you are close, it is time to move away about 10 feet. Now teach him to pivot on the forehand and face you with both eyes whenever you put visual or physical pressure (such as wiggling a lead rope) on his hips. The horse should begin to move consistently with you so that he begins circling as you walk around him.

Until the hindquarters consistently disengage and he smoothly pivots on the forehand, there is no point in undertaking much other work. Until he has learned to consistently keep both eyes on his handler, there is simply no way to command his attention. This is the hallmark of any learning: the horse stays focused on us and keeps both eyes on us wherever we move.

All safety maneuvers on horseback are based on disengaging the hindquarters. This removes the horse's primary means of propulsion and reduces his reactive drive. He cannot think his way out of a problem if he is focused only on blindly running away from it. So disengaging the hindquarters is the primary step in creating a momentary pause in his mind, where reflection and correction can occur. It is the first thing each horse must learn in order to be ready to go from round pen work to arena work.

Disengaging the hindquarters is the physical embodiment of the principle that we can only overcome fear and anxiety by action. The horse's impulse to run is not held in check by a more severe bit. It is displaced into the movement of rotating on the forehand and disengaging the hindquarters.

Franklin D. Roosevelt said in his first presidential inauguration address that "the only thing we have to fear is fear itself." The horse wants to bolt, to run as fast as his legs can carry him. If we can help him through that wave of overwhelming fear, even for just a moment or two, its grip on him will loosen, the fear will dissipate, and he can begin to think his way through his instinctive anxiety. Disengaging the hindquarters is the trick to helping him confront his instincts. And overcoming instinct is the key to getting a horse to be a safe riding companion.

The biggest problem I see with this maneuver is that, in fact, many times the rider is just as scared as the horse. The only way to overcome that reactive fear is to slowly and patiently rehearse disengaging the hindquarters on the ground and under saddle until it is second nature for both you and your horse. You must practice it so much that it becomes part of your and your horse's muscle memory. For starters, that means usually 10,000 repetitions or more. Practice trying to disengage the hindquarters incessantly, especially when something spooks your horse. You will have built in a physical mechanism to defuse and divert your horse's instinctual panic. The difference between a horse and a good horse is how quickly he can move from reacting instinctively out of fear to relying confidently on his training.

NEVER TAKE THE TRAIL FOR GRANTED.

▼

MOST PEOPLE ARE ANXIOUS to get their horse out on the trail. Don't be. That is the last place you want to go until you have put a lot of miles on your horse under saddle in the arena. The trail is a test of a horse's training. A deer might jump out of the woods. A barking dog can suddenly decide to aggressively hold his ground on the trail. A rattlesnake. A plastic bag. The real world — and all of its myriad unexpected manifestations — is out there, and you have to know you have created a safe, steady, well-balanced horse in which you can place a lot of trust. You would not take a test aircraft for its maiden voyage by flying into combat, so do not take a green horse out on the trail alone until he has become very seasoned and mature.

The first few times you and your horse venture out on the trail, it should always be in the company of a more dominant, seasoned trail horse. Nothing helps a junior, green horse more than watching a relaxed veteran take it all in stride. Try to get as many as 20 to 30 rides on the trail in the company of a seasoned string of trail horses before you consider taking your horse out alone. Then you can get to work developing good trail manners and gradually building his confidence that he can handle the trail without the accompaniment of other herd members.

That first trail ride alone is magic and memorable. It is as if your horse has graduated from college.

LEADERSHIP
IS DETERMINED
BY THE FOUR Cs.

▼

HORSES ARE ALWAYS SEARCHING for fair and effective leadership. A good leader exhibits the four Cs of leadership: *command, control, compassion,* and *communication.*

Command is a sense of awareness that takes in the needs of the herd. It ensures that the leader assesses all risks for the common good of the herd. A leader will always expose herself first to a danger, such as a coyote passing through a pasture, before allowing the herd to encounter the threat.

Control means the leader can move the other horses' feet. A leader exerts control. She can move the horses or stop them as she sees fit. If the coyote is off at a distance, the alpha mare will usually be the first to check out the threat with two or three senior mares coming up close behind while the rest of the herd is sent off to a safe distance. It also means the leader has thought ahead about where the herd should go and what the herd's response should be if the threat is deemed dangerous enough. It is a combination of forethought and execution.

A good experiment is to go out into a pasture with a group of horses that have bonded into a herd and introduce something novel into the pasture, like a large traffic cone or an empty wheelbarrow. Observe. You will always see the lead horse explore the threat first, before other herd members do. In the same fashion, the lead horse chooses what route to take, what pasture to eat in, and which water hole to use.

Compassion means the leader is always empathetic and sees the world through the eyes of the others in the herd. This is critical because each individual in the group sees the situation in a unique, personal context, and a good leader wants to account for these variable responses. It is making sure not that everyone responds the same way but that, despite individual differences, all the members respond as a team. This is why the alpha mare also learns to deftly direct traffic within the herd so that it responds as a unit if there appears to be a need to flee.

Communication refers specifically to how a leader instructs his horses clearly and succinctly — no wasted sounds, gestures, or energy. It also means clarity; things are spelled out for the herd in black and white. Everyone knows what is expected and what is needed to succeed. Again, the lead mare can direct herd members with a small toss or bobbing of the head. Her body also clearly communicates whether she remains on alert because she still is in doubt about a threat or she has relaxed because she has deemed it harmless.

Remember that leadership cannot be claimed. Exhibiting the four Cs will help you earn it, but in the end it's the herd that bestows the status of leader.

GIVE CREDIT.

▼

HORSEMANSHIP IS ABOUT HISTORY. It is about one generation of masters coming in with new ideas and techniques, and then a new generation coming along and apprenticing to the first set. A second and a third and a fourth generation of mentors take their place in turn. We are now in our fourth generation of trainers descended from the original founding fathers of natural horsemanship: namely, the Dorrance brothers, Bill and Tom, and Ray Hunt, Tom Dorrance's most brilliant student.

A good teacher is always stealing ideas and techniques from other clinicians. It is healthy, though, to recall from where and whom the ideas were lifted.

SPS:
SELF-PRAISE
STINKS.

▼

THE GREAT EQUINE CLINICIANS NEVER BRAG because they don't have to. The mediocre ones spend a lot of time telling you about their busy schedules, where they have been and where they are going, as if they are trying to impress you with how important and in demand they are. (I will forgive a little bit of advertising, but not too much.) The really bad ones brag about how good they are because no one else will.

Remember SPS: self-praise stinks. Just walk away from the braggarts. As a general rule, the humbler the teacher, the better he or she is. When passion and humility are united in the same horseman or horsewoman, that is a person worthy of your apprenticeship.

LEAD WITH
YOUR HEART.

▼

THE SIMPLEST DEFINITION OF A HERD is a band of individuals who are motivated to think of themselves as a group before they think of themselves as individuals. That would also be the definition of a good management group, a football team, an orchestra, a special ops force, an ordinary family, or any group we wanted to join if we had the choice. Developing that sense we call "being family" can be difficult, yet no state of grace satisfies us as much. Even our obituaries are largely devoted to listing the groups we belonged to during our lives rather than our individual accomplishments.

As predators, we were born to ride the knife edge, balancing between utter dependence on our own self-centered needs and the power of belonging to a group. The pull of the clan, our friendships at the chess club, the camaraderie of the fishing hole, or the closeness of a family holiday meal — those moments when we can set aside the sword of the self —are the happiest we will ever experience.

For horses, herd allegiance is simple: it is the way to survive longest and happiest. Dominance and hierarchy give the herd its structure.

Reliance on a mare as the leader ensures that herd members will not find themselves abandoned by a stallion who is suddenly caught up in stealing a mare from another harem or getting into a testosterone-fueled clash with another stud. An alpha mare, with her parental bond to the foals as well as the close consanguineous ties to other mares in the herd, is endowed with the power of family ties.

> *The alpha mare never makes a decision for herself.*
> *Her connectedness to the herd makes her almost*
> *incapable of it.*

She leads with her heart. She never makes a decision for herself; her connectedness makes her almost psychologically incapable of it. When the alpha mare orders the herd to move off in a certain direction or along a specific trail, there's never a question in the other members' minds that this is the best thing for all members of the herd.

When a horse is stalled in some maneuver, such as crossing a bridge or a tarp, I remind myself that if he sees the herd safely passing over the obstacle, he knows it is safe for him, too. I was once in Arizona's Saguaro National Park on my favorite trail horse, Sonny, just picking our way down one of the washes. Suddenly we heard the smack of a whip and the scream of a horse in pain a hundred yards ahead of us. We loped down to find a wrangler from a nearby ranch trying to get a new horse, a mint mustang, to walk through a tunnel below an underpass. The mustang would not go and the man was beating him mercilessly with a switch torn from a nearby tree.

I asked the guy to stop hitting his horse. I dismounted and walked Sonny two or three times back and forth under the underpass. Then I grabbed the mustang's reins and walked him on my left side with Sonny

"When I bestride him, I soar, I am a
hawk: he trots the air; the earth sings
when he touches it."

William Shakespeare, *Henry V*

on my right. The mustang ambled through without the slightest hesitation. The wrangler was dumbfounded: the power of the herd is something to behold.

As an astute acquaintance observed: "Horses like to be part of something bigger than themselves." In this age of enhanced spiritual awareness, we must understand that spirituality, in the broadest sense of the word, is the drive within humans as well to belong to something bigger than ourselves — something more significant, longer lasting, more enduring.

In the end, working for and with others makes us humans happiest.

A PHYSICAL CONFRONTATION IS A DEFEAT.

▼

A FULL-GROWN HORSE CAN WEIGH more than a thousand pounds. His muscles are far bigger and his nerves far better myelinated* than ours. He can react faster and more powerfully than you ever can. By definition, a physical confrontation with a horse is a losing (and, I might add, a dangerous) proposition. The only control a rider exerts over her horse is with her mind — not her arm or her leg or the bit or the whip.

If she scores a momentary physical victory, such as pulling the horse off-balance with the lead rope to make him move forward, he will not be impressed by her fairness. If that approach is all he sees, sooner or later he will counterreact, saying: "No, I think I will see what happens if I pull on you before you get to pull me off balance." You want the horse to trust you and sincerely believe in partnering up with you.

---

* Myelin is a lipid that insulates nerves, and the more myelin around the nerve, the faster it conducts. Why can't most human beings dodge a horse's foot when he kicks out? Because the horse's speed of reaction is faster than a human's, partly due to the greater amount of myelin around equine nerves.

At all costs, the rider must avoid pitting her strength against the horse's, because that scenario will only increase his motivation to challenge her. If a rider is getting into physical confrontations with her mount, it means that he is outsmarting her — not a good thing. As soon as a rider sees that things might get physical, she must change the scenario instantly.

The rider is always trying to demonstrate her good intentions to the horse. So getting into a physical confrontation with a horse is solid evidence something has gone wrong. It's time to rethink things or, better yet, get out of there and get some help before it dawns on the horse that he might be able to get the upper hand. When we are tempted to resort to brute strength, it is a warning we are approaching a breakdown in the relationship.

BEFORE DANGER STRIKES, CONSIDER THE POSSIBILITIES.

▼

ORSES CAN BE DANGEROUSLY REACTIVE, explosively powerful, and notoriously unpredictable. When they spook or panic, they can easily kill a person. Don't be fearful, but do be cautious. At all times, a good handler is looking at how to keep herself safe. This means triangulating in your mind, almost as a matter of reflex: Where will my horse most likely go when he bolts? Have I left him a way out that does not involve running over or through me?

Get in the habit of identifying the most likely ways in which an unexpected threat might come. Which direction is the wind blowing? Where is traffic routed? Could other nearby horses suddenly bolt? A horse can easily panic if others do.

Half of safety is considering the possibilities; the other half is taking reasonable precautions. The biggest danger comes from taking the horse for granted and not respecting the prey-driven instincts the species has developed over 40 million years of evolution.

AVOID IDLENESS; EMPLOY STILLNESS.

▼

THEODORE ROOSEVELT SAID: "Black care rarely sits behind a rider whose pace is fast enough." He was referring to the emotional and psychological benefits of throwing oneself into action.

Horses look for action, too. Like any other reasonably intelligent creature, they need a job that keeps them active so they are physically and mentally engaged. Horses who work on ranches are the lucky ones. They have full-time, steady employment. They are on the move all day long, constantly thinking, and immersed in work.

It's not the work per se. Horses need a mission, a purpose to make them feel fulfilled, just as we do. Most horses are, as one trainer put it, "over-bred, overfed, and underrode." A horse's job could be pushing cattle, taking his rider on a trail ride, or carrying a child in equine-assisted learning. It will keep him sharp, focused, and content. It is when horses sit around that we see them lose their socialization skills and get fat, lazy, and pushy.

Look for ways keep your horse's mind and body occupied. You will have an engaged, fulfilled partner.

There is a difference between stillness and shutting down. Stillness is a mindful pause in action, like the silence between notes in music. Stillness defines action. The duality is what brings them into being.

Shutting down, on the other hand, is the gradual decay or outright loss of energy. Horses epitomize this principle in two ways. First, since the energy from the handler interacts with the energy from horse, calm is the antithesis of action. In fact, we use the stilling of the handler's body to stop a horse. It means we ask nothing of the horse, and he will grow still or even go to sleep.

Inactivity is tranquility. But sustained too long, it can turn into the equivalent of sleeping one's time away. We all know stories of the 65-year-old gentleman who got his gold watch, retired, and then dropped dead three months later because he had not given himself "a new job" after stepping down from full-time employment.

Inactivity kills the soul. Idleness provides the opening for depression, and action is the antidote for melancholy.

TO BE HEARD,
WHISPER.

▼

EW SITUATIONS ARE MORE STRESSFUL than calling an emergency
response team to the bedside of a patient who has just suffered a
cardiac arrest. The adrenaline in the air is palpable — and conta-
gious. As a physician, I've learned never to run to a code. The staff on the
floor has already initiated CPR and ventilation, so I want to arrive at the
scene calm and collected: no perspiring, no panting, and no heaving.

As everyone is shouting, I walk in and begin speaking in a slow, quiet
voice. I do it because a quiet voice is like a quiet body; it drains energy to
a lower state. It compels others to quiet down and keep commotion to a
minimum so the team can hear my orders for the code. Suddenly the tenor
of the room changes. Anxiety level falls.

Loud voices, big gestures, and "large and in charge" body language are
only signs of an individual struggling for control. This person feels that if
his words alone cannot convince others, then packaging them with high
emotion should do the trick. Think of a drill sergeant dressing down new
recruits. It is meant to be assaultive and intimidating.

Horses teach us that we can hear and be heard better when our voices are calm and deliberate. Think of the voice of a pilot. Even under the most stressful of situations, pilots pride themselves on exuding an orderly and commanding calm. President Theodore Roosevelt believed that his policy of American diplomacy could be summed up in the proverb "Speak softly but carry a big stick." The corollary? "If you shout, your stick can't be very big."

OVERCOME WITH LEVERAGE, NOT RESISTANCE.

▼

WHEN YOU ENCOUNTER RESISTANCE, look for leverage to turn it into a curve of compromise. Resist the temptation to create resistance in response to resistance.

A perfect example is how you use your reins. To control leverage and avoid resistance, first learn to ride with an emphasis on one rein, not both. You can switch from the left to the right, but avoid working both reins at once to prevent a muscle contest with the horse.

While a horse is relatively calm, he will permit a rider to control his movements with bilateral pressure on the bit. Riders do it all the time, of course. If, however, someone or something spooks a horse, even the strongest rider would have a tough time trying to pull him to a stop with two hands on the bit. He is so powerful that he can easily overpower the rearward pressure the rider exerts.

For this reason, it is valuable to work our horse under saddle with one rein or the other. Always apply pressure to the bit asymmetrically. If a rider pulls on the bit from only one side, she will regain control of the horse because the asymmetric pressure gives the rider leverage — something the horse cannot really overcome. This is because the more he is pulled into a circling maneuver, the more his hips begin to disengage. As the circle gets tighter and tighter, it is more difficult for him to apply power to his rear end. So the horse's headlong plunge straight ahead is turned with leverage into a curve — a circle. The circle gets tighter and brings him to a stop.

With practice, it will take less and less leverage to get the circling response and disengage the hindquarters. This emphasis on lateral flexion automatically translates into vertical flexion at the poll — the top of the head — without having to fuss to control the horse's head position with both reins.

Anytime the sense of a great effort or exertion inserts itself, it is a sign that fear or haste (or both) has somehow inserted itself into our technique. The hallmark of control is ease and low energy. The struggle for control means we've already lost it.

THE MORE A HORSE SPOOKS, THE LESS AFRAID HE BECOMES.

▼

F EAR IS A TOUGH EMOTION to deal with because it literally short-circuits thinking — in humans and in horses. All creatures' brains are wired so that panic trumps cognition. On the surface, we think that the way to control fear is to suppress it. It's not. Fear can only be approached when the actual moment of fear has passed. It needs to be defused. We do that by removing ourselves — or our horse — from the source of fear.

Whenever a horse spooks, he is telling you, "Hey, I need help. I have a problem and I'm going to need some guidance to get through this." Do not think of it as an alarm as much as a plea for help. Every time your horse spooks, he is giving you valuable information about what shuts down the thinking side of his brain and unleashes the reactive, instinctive side of his brain.

The more we are willing to tackle the spooks, the less reactive our horse will become. The more we imprint upon him that he can successfully think his way through a problem, the more he will fulfill that promise.

Fear arises from a lack of understanding, from the lack of a plan for coping with it. The remedy is to practice handling fear by coming at the feared object obliquely, so we pass near it and then move off. Come around and pass near it again, and then move past it. Gradually, the horse will learn to glide past it. It is conquered not through confrontation, but through sublimation.

LEADERS ASSUME THE RISK FOR ALL.

▼

L EADERSHIP AND AUTHORITY ARE NOT ABOUT POWER. G. K. Ches-
terton, the British author and critic, wrote: "If a rhinoceros were to
enter . . . now, there is no denying he would have great power here.
But I should be the first to rise and assure him that he had no authority
whatever." Leadership's power is derived by a combination of authority,
inspiration, and empathy.

When I first introduce a horse to something scary, such as tethered
balloons blowing on a windy day, I never ask him to do anything more than
walk with me around the object. I always put myself closest to the danger
and leave my horse on the outside where he has plenty of room to bolt to
freedom. We walk around with no pressure, making circles back and forth,
always with the danger nearest to me. Doing this long enough and patiently
enough so the horse generates little or no anxiety makes the task easy.

Leadership comprises so many combinations of qualities, circumstances, and charisma. Yet one common characteristic of leaders is the

ability to understand what works, and what is trivial and unimportant in securing a desired outcome.

Former secretary of state Colin Powell wrote: "Great leaders are almost always great simplifiers, who can cut through argument, debate, and doubt to offer a solution everybody can understand."* It is not just the solution. It is silencing the issues that obscure the objective and drain resolve.

In the herd, the alpha mare must prove to the herd every day that she will always put the interests of the herd before her own and display courage in the face of threat, putting herself in harm's way first. As a veteran of Operation Desert Storm, I was stirred by the film *We Were Soldiers* (Paramount Pictures, 2002), about the real-life events surrounding the Battle of La Drang in Vietnam in November 1965. Before Lt. Col. Harold G. "Hal" Moore and the 17th Battalion of the Seventh Cavalry departed for what would later be called "the Valley of Death," one of the bloodiest encounters of the war, Moore spoke to his men. He said to them: "This I swear before you and before Almighty God: that when we go into battle, I will be the first to set foot on the field, and I will be the last to step off. And I will leave *no one* behind. Dead or alive, we will all come home together. So help me God."

Exposing oneself to the hazards that the whole group will face, sharing their fate, and assuring each and every member that the leader is honor-bound to face the dangers — first and last — for them, is what the herd demands.

* Oren Harari, *The Leadership Secrets of Colin Powell* (McGraw-Hill, 2002).

LOYALTY IS NEVER CONVENIENT.

▼

"LOYALTY CANNOT BE BLUEPRINTED," Maurice Franks, an attorney and activist, wrote. "It cannot be produced on an assembly line. In fact, it cannot be manufactured at all, for its origin is the human heart — the center of self-respect and human dignity. It is a force which leaps into being only when conditions are exactly right for it."

When following a leader or sticking by a friend puts a person at risk, that is when loyalty is expressed. Along with honesty, it is the most noble and noteworthy of human traits.

The profound partnership between humans and their horses requires loyalty, a willingness to put the integrity of that relationship before all other obligations. In a friendship at this deep level, horse and human become family. They are bound together for life.

When I reach that depth of loyalty with a horse, I breathe a deep sigh of relief because I know I will never endanger our relationship to impress someone else or to make a point. Horses do not know the meaning of deceit. They will never betray you. I know our relationship is safe until the end of our days.

In 1914, when World War I broke out, my grandfather was a cavalry officer in the Austro-Hungarian Empire. My grandmother was worried sick about him going off to war. He reassured her that nothing would go wrong as long as he and his great warhorse, Otto, were together. He was right. He and Otto made it through two long years of combat.

But in 1916, as my grandfather's unit was ordered to charge over a hill and descend on a unit of infantry, they were met by horrendous mortar fire. Shells exploded all around them. Otto, true to his training, reared up and took the full brunt of one of the mortar's explosions. My grandfather crawled to his side and saw that three of his four limbs had been torn off, his belly had been ripped open, and he was partially eviscerated. My grandfather dispatched him with a bullet.

He never let us forget that everyone in our family owed our lives to Otto. He kept a photo of Otto on his desk until the day he died. He once admitted to me, "Yes, the Bible tells us that we must love our fellow man, so we do. But I, for one, would rather love a horse because he has proved himself to be so much more worthy of my love and loyalty than most men that I have met."

We don't think about cultivating the habit of loyalty, but we should. It means we strive always to resist the temptation to gossip. It means we always do our best to keep our word and meet our commitments to that person. It means we give that person the benefit of the doubt when others cast aspersions until all sides are heard and carefully weighed. It means, to paraphrase comedian Gary Moore, we become that one person who walks into the room to stand beside a friend when everyone else is walking out to abandon him.

"Man is lost and is wandering in
a jungle where real values have
no meaning. Real values can have
meaning to man only when he steps
on to the spiritual path, a path where
negative emotions have no use."

Sai Baba

HORSEMANSHIP TRANSFORMS.

▼

ORSES USUALLY START OFF LIFE JUST FINE. They have a good understanding of what it means to be a horse. Later, as they grow and mature, they may begin to develop people problems. We humans aggravate the problems because we tend to bring our emotional baggage into the round pen or the arena with us and visit it upon the horse in myriad forms.

What the horse really needs is for us to discipline ourselves to leave all that stuff outside the gate. We must focus only on his responses. He will quickly remind us when we drift back into our own thoughts and issues.

The horse makes demands on us. Working with him motivates us to develop better concentration and to turn our energies elsewhere than inward, on ourselves. That is a good thing. He teaches us that multitasking may have a place in the office but never in the barn. In order to develop the impeccable intention demanded of a horseman or horsewoman, we must learn to focus our attention on one thing and to keep the rest of life from intruding on our purpose.

These lessons translate to the round pen or the living room. When you are having a conversation with a loved one, are you truly focused on what they are telling you, or do you let other thoughts and distractions intrude? Do you check your text messages? Do you simply listen to hear them take a breath so you can insert your own opinions? Ask yourself: Am I listening to the conversation with complete focus and no agenda?

The master horseman or horsewoman looks for every opportunity to extend the mastery of the round pen into the other aspects of life.

ENERGY *and* EMOTION

When we see that energy and emotion can be truly independent of each other, we can begin to master both. We can employ energy to our purpose without getting angry or defensive or excited or manipulative. And we can choose where to place our emotions, to avoid spending them foolishly. This changes the question from "How angry must I be to get a response?" to "How much energy must I exert to make this happen?"

COMBINING ENERGY AND EMOTION IS A CHOICE.

▼

WE LIVE IN A WORLD WHERE THERE IS ENERGY IN US, and we share that energy between ourselves and all the life-forms around us.

We bring that energy into focus by harnessing our *attention*. We shape our attention with our *intention,* to bring about change. When we learn to use that intention impeccably, it becomes the vehicle for the expression of our purpose or our will in the physical realm.

We can induce changes when our energy is properly harnessed by our intention. This works most effectively when it remains uncluttered by emotion. We achieve this clarity by learning to summon our attention without attachment.

That is a tall order for people because, as predators, it runs contrary to our nature. As hunters and fighters, we are programmed to package energy and emotion together. Think about how anger enables us to summon massive amounts of energy.

The horse gives us a different perspective on energy and emotion. He is expert at reading the visceral and intuitive energy we give off subconsciously in our body posture, head position, and hand gestures. He will always try to read our energetic intention, but the message can get garbled when mixed with emotion.

Pure intention is energy; emotion, on the other hand, reflects appetites, needs, and ambitions. The horse can become confused because we jack up our emotions when we really mean to summon more energy. So instead of simply perceiving more energy in play, he is also reading, say, anger or frustration. We clutter up our energy.

The horse's important lesson becomes: "Stop! You don't need to stir emotion and energy together." In fact, our energy works far more effectively when it is emotionally neutral and drained of any reactive association.

We can learn from the horse to be more mindful of the play of our energy in our daily lives. For example, we may ask him to accelerate from a walk to a trot. Often, I will see students start yelling as they get after the horse when, in fact, that confuses him. He is perfectly willing to respond to an energetic signal, but when we holler at him to get going he is confused by the sudden aggression. So he teaches us self-control — to overcome our instinct to get aggressive and instead draw on our reserves of energy.

Mindlessly yoking energy and emotion together is exhausting, depleting, and unhealthy. We must show respect for energy — our own and that of others — by pacing ourselves and using it sparingly. We want to transmit energy in as pure and discrete a form as possible. No judgment. Not good or bad. Not happy or sad. Just effective.

The quality of energy should not depend on outcomes. Think of your vital energy as the gas pedal in your car. If you are pouring on the gas in a moment of road rage, you are not accelerating to get up a hill or steer out of a curve. You're mad; you've let your emotions hijack your energy.

Apply the gas without emotion. When we summon more energy to address a need, we should ask ourselves: Do we want to apply this much energy to this problem? Or did we unintentionally let emotion creep in?

We can train ourselves to summon emotion by choice, not by default.

TO KNOW
WHEN TO RELEASE
IS TO KNOW WHY.

▼

WE MUST ALWAYS UNDERSTAND "THE WHY" of what we are teaching the horse. Knowing "the why" shapes the timing, and the timing reveals "the how."

For example, if a rider wants to teach her horse to back up, the first step is to teach him to pick up his front foot because that is the initial movement required in backing up. The rider's intent should be to release the horse as soon as he first lifts his foot. In fact, the rider should sense the moment when her horse is *thinking* about picking up his foot because the moment of release will happen as the foot leaves the ground.

Many riders try to learn techniques by rote, but no one can develop an impeccable release from a recipe. Impeccable release stems from a profound understanding of the horse's nature, and why and when he will respond. Study every movement, every gesture of the horse, until you profoundly understand how and what he is thinking.

ENERGY
IS DUALITY.

▼

ENERGY IS ALWAYS IN A STATE OF FLUX, morphing between static and dynamic forms. Static energy is applied with a fixed intensity. If I simply lay the length of my calf along the side of my horse to make him soften his flank and elevate his rib cage, that is static energy. I do not change the intensity I apply.

Dynamic or driving energy is a pulsatile, rhythmic form of energy, rising crescendo-style, then dropping, then rising again in a rapid, percussive style. If my horse will not soften his flank with the just pressure of my calf against him, then I can pulse him with my heel (or even my spur if I am wearing it). The rhythmic, wave-like pulsations are more forceful and therefore more difficult for a horse to ignore or resist than static energy. Driving energy will compel a horse to yield more quickly.

By the same token, we can break our own energy down into passive and active forms. When our energy is passive, it is at its lowest state — drained out of our body and deposited in the ground. I sometimes call this my "bus stop slump." I imagine standing at a bus stop and there is not a bus in sight. My shoulders are stooped and my head is down. But when my bus comes along, my body fills with energy. It goes active: "Hey, wait a minute! That's my bus! Over here!" My body has become energized. It wants something to happen.

Or imagine someone standing peacefully behind you in a queue. Your body is tranquil, in a low, passive energy state. Now someone tries to break into line in front of you. Your body is instantly activated, energized. We need to observe how it feels to assume a passive energy signature as opposed to consciously trying to make something happen, to effect change. Our horse will know this before we do.

Dynamic energy cannot exist without a basis in static energy, and activity cannot be shaped unless it arises from passivity.

THE GROUND IS CLOSEST TO THE TRUTH.

▼

I T MUST BE IN OUR GENES. We see a horse and immediately want to throw a leg up and ride it. We are sometimes downright foolhardy when it comes to mounting a horse and trusting it to go immediately out on the trail. There are a couple of good reasons to compel you to linger on the ground.

First, the relationship between human and horse is most meaningful to the horse on the ground. There, two species are interacting using their body language, partners dancing together in a choreography of energetic initiatives. When the person climbs on a horse's back, everything changes to indirect communication. Weight shifts. We apply leg pressure and bit pressure. Why? Once you are on the horse's back, he can no longer read your energy and your body language directly. In fact, you are sitting right in the large blind spot behind his head. Granted, he can look upward out of the side of his eye, but under saddle he must sense you indirectly.

Second, anything that does not work consistently on the ground will never translate well under saddle. In fact, it will always get worse if the foundational work on the ground is not solid. It can only deteriorate when the horse has to deal with the indirect signals from his rider while balancing the added burden of carrying her.

All difficulties in horsemanship begin on the ground or end there.

The rule is simple: Stay on the ground until the lesson is virtually perfect, then try it under saddle. The corollary is: If it is not working well under saddle, get back on the ground.

A friend of mine once said, "I've found that the more I get thrown out of the saddle to the ground, the more demanding and refined my ground-work technique becomes." That is the hard way (literally) to learn the value of partnering with your horse on the ground. All difficulties in horsemanship begin on the ground or end there.

ENERGY
IS STICKY.

▼

ENERGY HAS CERTAIN PROPERTIES, and one of them is that it gets sticky when it stops moving. It is a bit like rolling a heavy barrel. It can take a lot of effort to start it moving, but once under way it picks up speed, and then it requires substantially less energy to continue. Letting a horse stand in place, on the other hand, or petting him too many times for too long, will make him stick to the spot. Once he gets stuck, it will take far more energy to get him moving again.

A good rider will get her horse moving before applying intention. Once he is flowing, it requires far less energy to teach him. A moving horse is a lot more willing than a standing one.

Stopping, resting, and taking a break are all fine. We take complete responsibility for the energy we engender. Say I decide to take a break and have an affectionate moment with my horse in the shade. I am mindful of bringing my horse into the shade and let him "stick" to the spot. I am intentionally grounding our energy, letting it drain into the ground. It is quite another matter, though, if it is my *intention* to have my horse circling at the trot and I just let him simply slow to walk and then stumble to a stop and then go up and pet him.

A moving horse is a lot more willing than a
standing one.

To the master teacher, an impeccable moment is one in which intention is totally and perfectly expressed. Nothing is left undone or carried out improperly.

An impeccable session is a string of impeccable moments. And an impeccable life — enlightenment — is an uninterrupted stream of flawlessness. Enlightenment is rarely achieved because it requires such an unrelenting demand of energetic focus. But focusing on enlightenment, fostering the habit of mindfulness, is a prerequisite for enhancing well-being and contentment in one's life.

GROW BEYOND
INSTINCT.

▼

O UR FUNDAMENTAL NATURE IS A GIVEN. It is written. It is largely genetically determined, and railing against fate is a waste of time. What we can do is become adept at modifying our instinctual responses. That is the true measure of discipline and self-control. The shorter the gap between the innate, reflexive action and the well-thought-out, deliberate response, the greater the power of the warrior.

Horses have their own brand of wisdom. Because they are prey animals, flight is their primary defense, and it is critical to their sense of security to be free to move their feet.

I had a buckskin filly named Pepper who, most of the time, was fine but would flip out upon discovering she was tied to a rail. It was as if she unexpectedly glimpsed the true terror of the situation and would go berserk, pulling back with all her might. She could rip hitching posts out of the ground. Once she reared and flipped completely over on her back.

I told myself, "I'm a horse trainer. I can teach this horse to stand still." I launched into my usual routine, working with Pepper when she was tired and gradually desensitizing her. When I tested her to see if she would spook and pull back, she stood there cool as a cucumber, looking completely cured. I patted myself on the back, pleased that I had finally fixed the problem.

Then, a few months down the road, and without warning, Pepper exploded again.

I started reflecting on what really spooked her: the fact that she couldn't escape. So what would happen if she were never tied up?

"What?" I thought to myself. "I've spent half my life teaching people to tie their horse to the rail with a slipknot, and now I'm going to give in to Pepper and not tie her up at all?"

I hope you can tell what was wrong with my thinking: "I'm going to *give in* to Pepper . . . " No, Pepper wasn't trying to force me to surrender; she was trying to show me something new. I started playing around with the lead rope, just looping it once around the metal hitching post. When she spooked, she pulled back and met virtually no resistance. She backpedaled, and then she stopped reacting.

Periodically, something would happen and Pepper would return to her panic reaction. Eventually, she learned that there was nothing, ever, holding her back. She finally calmed down and could think her way through the problem.

Human civilization and culture demonstrate, to a large extent, society's collective ability to move to beyond instinct and into the realm of creative thinking. We don't accomplish this by fighting or suppressing our personalities. We acknowledge that we are born with or develop certain traits over which we have little or no control. That is our makeup, but each of us is responsible for thinking our way past those shortcomings.

The desire to dedicate our lives to this task is what makes us heroic. The ability to do it as a society is what makes us civilized.

RHYTHMIC MOVEMENT IS PREDICTABLE ENERGY.

▼

W̲E ARE CREATURES OF HABIT. The reason it is hard to change the status quo is that we are comfortable with it. The human organism is designed to plan and organize so that life does not offer us any unwelcome or potentially disastrous changes.

Rhythm, however, helps us accept change.

Horses appreciate rhythm. Energy that comes in a rhythm means the crescendo of the wave of energy is predictable. Adding a rhythmic, pulsatile character to our energy can allow us to drive or move a horse with less work than it takes to sustain static energy.

In the natural world, almost everything with the power to change has a rhythm — a beat, a pulse, a wave — from the ocean to the human heart. Although energy can be applied as a sustained, unwavering presence, like a dead tree lying across a stream, static energy is more likely to create

"The goal of life is to make your heartbeat match the beat of the universe, to match your nature with Nature."

Joseph Campbell

resistance than change. Sudden, unexpected, and explosive energy, on the other hand — a lightning bolt, an earthquake, a punishment — is disruptive and untrustworthy and brings about dramatic and often destructive transformation.

But energy applied with rhythm, pace, and predictability — like the waves on the beach — is at the heart of purposeful change. We know it and recognize it as such immediately.

BREAKING
THROUGH

The problem we notice on the surface is almost never the real dilemma, which is often deeply embedded in history. We have to take a step, sometimes many steps, backward to discover where the trouble started. Once we truly "see" the problem, we can then advance imaginative and diverse strategies for tackling it.

THERE IS
NO BEST WAY.

▼

FIFTY YEARS AGO THE ACCEPTED METHOD to accustom a horse to being saddled was to snub him up to a post, cinch the saddle tight, and let him buck his brains out until he accepted it. It worked, but deep down the horse never completely trusted that saddle.

We no longer believe in such methods. We sack our horses out. We get them used to a cinch, then a bareback pad, then a light saddle, then a working saddle. It is the best method — for now.

When working with horses, there is no best way, one way, right way, or wrong way to do things. Period. Whoever insists that his way is best has a lot to learn. The world is full of horsemen and horsewomen coming up with new and better ways to train horses. Horsemanship is built upon a rich history of innovations, so sooner or later the best way to do something with a horse no longer is.

Always keep an open mind that the next person — or horse — to come along just might be able to teach you something new and better.

TO CONQUER PROBLEMS, IMAGINE SOLUTIONS.

▼

OMETIMES I AM DUMBFOUNDED THAT AN OWNER or handler will ask for a specific solution to a specific problem with a horse — as if there is some library where someone has catalogued every solution to every problem that ever existed in a horse. Yep, the answer is on the second floor, third stack, filed under "One-eyed horses that crib* during total eclipses of the moon."

Only you, as the owner, have the most specific experience and information about your horse — just as with a parent and a child. Use your imagination to see how you might approach a specific problem with your horse rather than believing that there is someone out there with the magic silver bullet that will explain it all for you. Horsemanship is hard work — not because the techniques can be difficult, but because each horse

---

* Cribbing is a complex compulsive behavior where a horse grabs, say, the stall door with his teeth, pulls back and sucks air.

requires a unique, inventive approach. Imagination is just as important as experience when working with a horse.

Horsemanship demands creativity. Use your powers of invention to deconstruct the horse's problem. Let's go back to my earlier example of Sonny, the Quarter Horse who is deathly afraid of water. I could ask myself: How big a puddle will he fear? Is he afraid of one that is 4 inches wide? Well, why not? So Sonny is telling me that one potential approach that I could use would be to start slowly working on the size of the puddle since there is a minimum size at which the puddle ceases to be a problem.

Imagination is how you deconstruct problems. Deconstructing problems is how you solve them. The horse's problems are hardly ever insurmountable, but lack of imagination can make them seem so.

DON'T FIX PROBLEMS; CHANGE THEM.

▼

A S PREDATORS, WE TEND TO CHARGE RIGHT AT PROBLEMS. Even our nomenclature betrays our innate aggressiveness while problem solving. We talk of "tackling" or "cracking" a problem. We even say "cut to the chase."

Don't run at problems. Walk up to them. Approach them obliquely, with finesse.

The greatest gift a handler can bring to her horse is creativity — and particularly when it comes to deconstructing a problem to resolve it. Mike, a friend of mine, had a horse that was very skittish around diesel tractors. He decided that he would always turn on the tractor before feeding time. The sound of a Ford 3600 diesel took on an entirely new meaning for the horse. The rumbling of the engine became music to his ears!

On the surface, the problem appeared to be desensitizing the horse to the sound of the tractor. But the answer lay in ensuring that the noise took on a positive connotation: dinnertime! Sometimes the things you think should work simply do not, and then you must be ready to create a fresh approach. A creative approach.

Look at problems obliquely and avoid becoming fixated on a "one problem–one answer" response. Instead, deconstruct the problem and evaluate multiple solutions. Try them out and look for the one that is the most elegant and the least energetically demanding for you and your horse.

"When an ordinary man attains knowledge, he is a sage; when a sage attains understanding, he is an ordinary man."

Zen saying

TACKLE SMALL PROBLEMS BEFORE THEY BECOME BIG ONES.

▼

EVERY TIME OUR HORSE SHIES AWAY OR SPOOKS, he is telling us we need to address a problem. When we walk around or avoid a small problem, it grows exponentially into a big one. When we see the first hint of an issue, we must make a commitment to our horse that we will fix it. If we attack problems when they are small, they never have an opportunity to become major ones.

For example, someone you supervise is starting to habitually arrive late to the office. The sooner you sit down and say, "In the future, I would like you to call when you think you are going to be late," the sooner that person will have to monitor himself to avoid having to call you all the time.

Similarly, often owners will see their horses become uncomfortable, agitated, or even outright aggressive in an effort to avoid something that frightens them. Instead, however, of immediately setting to work on outlining the problem, discovering the triggers and creating solutions, owners go into avoidance mode. They recognize the triggers but develop methods or rules to avoid setting them off. Things like "Just don't touch his ears" or "Always come up to him with the blanket off to your left side" or "Never turn the pressure all the way up in the hose because it makes a hissing noise."

Learn to be grateful whenever your horse reveals an issue to you. Rejoice when such issues are still small, and address them early so they can be cleared out of your horse's life once and for all.

TRY THE 180-DEGREE SOLUTION.

▼

HORSES SEEM TO KNOW *precisely* when we are running behind schedule. That is when they decide not to enter the trailer. Things are guaranteed to go haywire because we are in a hurry, so people often bring their horses to a trainer to reteach the art of trailering.

Whenever I am stuck on a problem I ask, "What if I turn the question upside down?" It can produce a dramatic shift in focus — what I call the "180-degree solution." Here, instead of teaching the horse to get into the trailer, we teach him to get out. Every time he puts one foot in the trailer, we back him out. Two feet, back him out. Three feet, four feet, and so on.

This takes care of the horse's primary concern: feeling trapped in the confines of that box. Instead he thoroughly understands the way out. The way in becomes trivial!

So often, problem solving involves turning the question on its head. Then the answer may just shake out in front of you.

LOVE IS NEVER THE PROBLEM.

▼

I WILL SAY UNAPOLOGETICALLY that I love my horses, just as my grandfather did. In my partnerships with horses I have wrestled with how to express that love more fully. The lesson that horses bring to life for me is that I must work to enhance my sense of communion with other life-forms around me, animal and human alike.

I believe we once felt this immediate and palpable intimacy with all of nature. We were immersed in it and we trusted it. With the onset of the Industrial Revolution and the dawning of our Digital Age, however, we have been drawn away from that primary sense of connectivity. In a very real sense, we have banished ourselves from the natural world with all its wonders.

I believe the horse's greatest gift to us is the knowledge that, while that sense of closeness may have atrophied, it still lies dormant within each of us and can be awakened anytime we choose. He constantly tries to teach us that we can reestablish our unity with the world around us.

We need to free our hearts of any doubt that we are energetically interconnected. Without a sense of relatedness, we run the risk of forgetting the meaning of the remarkable photograph of our Earth taken during the last Apollo mission to the moon. The splendor of that beautiful "blue marble" in space is a magnificent image of how life is bound together by its underlying unity.

Henry David Thoreau wrote during his stay at Walden Pond: "I went to the woods because I wished to live deliberately, to confront only the essential facts of life, and see if I could learn what it had to teach, and not, when I came to die, discover that I had not lived." The partnership we feel with our horses is a fundamental, tangible assertion that we can make a profound reconnection. It is our birthright. We have only to reclaim it to regain the earthly paradise that has been given to us. The voice of the herd is undeniable and unmistakable.

EPILOGUE

There is still time for a predator to turn to the herd.

The horse's prey mind believes in the "we" of the herd, an egalitarian notion of the common good of the group. Membership is more motivating than selfishness. Inclusion in the group is more important than identification of the self. This sense of communion derives from an awareness of connectivity.

On the other hand, the psyche of the predator asserts the primacy of the "me." This is the fundamental faith that success ultimately rests on the principle that there are limited resources and these must be secured in a competitive, if not outright hostile, environment. Where herd members derive part of their character from the cohesiveness of the herd, human beings derive it from the notion of autobiographical isolation, of an ego that separates the psyche from everything else. The herd establishes an intimate connectivity while the predatory view insists on differentiation.

Global awareness will be required in a world increasingly crippled by planet-wide threats rather than regional ones. The escalating threat of pandemics like the Ebola virus will inevitably impose a new consciousness that what tragedy befalls my neighbor is also my tragedy, his children are my children, his herd is my herd.

The prey view is compelling. It offers us hope that the common good may present us with as much satisfaction and security as did our earliest, primeval appetites, and that we could frame our survival not in terms of predation and consumption, but in terms of stewardship and charity.

Perhaps, because we have been so deeply touched by horses, we may prove ourselves more willing to ride down a different path, to veer off onto a different trajectory. Where our human herd will travel, where our footsteps will next carry us, is simply a question of where we will place our faith and how we choose to live.

Albert Schweitzer, winner of the Nobel Peace Prize, summed it up when he asserted that we must all strive to live ethical lives. He wrote: "A man is ethical only when life, as such, is sacred to him, that of plants and animals as that of his fellow men, and when he devotes himself helpfully to all life that is in need of help."

The way of the herd, the faith of the horse, all lie on the path to goodness and grace.

ACKNOWLEDGMENTS

No one ever gives thanks to all the people he should.

That said, I first want to thank all the wonderful horses in my life. There have been so many, but some I consider family: Ace, Andy, Sonny, Mahto, Romeo, and Pepper.

Second, I must express my gratitude to my grandfather, Hans Ornstein, who helped raise me and passed his great love of horses on to me.

Third, my family. My wife, Jane, has always supported me in my love of horses. She has sacrificed so many things in her own life to ensure I could accomplish more in my life with horses. She has never ceased to amaze me with her skills as a clinical psychologist and how magically she can apply them in equine-assisted therapy. Jane continually inspires me to believe there are always greater emotional depths to be plumbed with a horse. She has steadfastly believed in my dreams, even when they were not her own. Her hard work has allowed my family and me to spend an enchanted life at our horse ranch in Tucson, Arizona.

I also want to thank my three children: Josh, Luke, and Tessa. Although not one of my children ever got infected with the "horse bug," they nonetheless respected how much I got out of my life spent training horses and staunchly supported me in my dedication to training them. The presence of my children was the largest factor in ensuring that our family life at the ranch was always uplifting, inspiring, and fun.

I have had so many wonderful teachers and mentors in the world of horses. To name a few: Monty Roberts, John and Josh Lyons, Pat and Linda Parelli, Clinton Anderson, Lanny Leach, Barbara Rector, Christie Metz, and Marc Devereaux.

I am fortunate to have had a wonderful team of trainers, horse professionals, and wranglers at Rancho Bosque. I am indebted to every one of them who "rode for the brand." Running herd over all of us is Linda Parker, who keeps the ranch humming like a Swiss clock and keeps us all humble.

I am indebted to my literary agents, Mike Larsen and Elizabeth Pomada, who never fail to inspire me and move me on to the next manuscript.

Finally, I thank the family of friends at Storey Publishing, especially Deb Burns. Storey is a group of inspired individuals who have long believed that the message horses convey can help all of us lead better lives. They have always endorsed the notion that the community of man, animal, and plants constitutes a fundamental harmony of happiness if we can only learn how to access it.

ALLAN J. HAMILTON, MD,
is a neurosurgeon, a horse trainer, a developer of
equine-assisted learning programs, and the author
of *Zen Mind, Zen Horse*. A medical script consultant
for the hit television series *Grey's Anatomy*, he raises
horses on a ranch in Tucson, Arizona.

Also by Allan J. Hamilton, MD